RIVER SAFETY ANTHOLOGY

THE AMERICAN CANOE ASSOCIATION'S

RIVER

SAFETY

ANTHOLOGY

Charlie Walbridge
and Jody Tinsley

Illustrated by Leigh Ellis

MENASHA RIDGE PRESS
BIRMINGHAM, ALABAMA

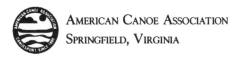
AMERICAN CANOE ASSOCIATION
SPRINGFIELD, VIRGINIA

Illustrations by Leigh Ellis
Cover design by Grant Tatum
Text design by Carolina Graphics Group

Cataloging-in-Publication Data
Walbridge, Charles C., 1948–
    The American Canoe Association's river safety anthology: accounts of rescue
and tragedy on North American rivers/by Charlie Walbridge, Jody Tinsley.
        p. cm.
    ISBN 0-89732-192-8
    1. White-water canoeing–North America–Case studies. 2. Canoeing accidents–
North America–Case studies. 3. Rescues–North America–Case studies. I. Tinsley,
Jody, 1964- . II. American Canoe Association. III. Title.
    GV776.5.W35   1995
    797.1'22–dc20   95-35996
                                                                        CIP

Menasha Ridge Press   American Canoe Association
700 South 28th Street   7432 Alban Station Boulevard
Suite 206   Suite B-226
Birmingham, AL 35233   Springfield, VA 22150
(800) 247-9437   (703) 451-0141
www.menasharidge.com   www.aca-paddler.org

To all paddlers who have lost their lives
doing what they loved best—running rivers.

INTRODUCTION

Whitewater rivers are exciting, ever-changing, and marvelous. They allow us to travel through unspoiled surroundings, to test our skills, and to spend time with friends. While risk is an important component of running rapids, the sport is surprisingly safe and an average paddler may never encounter a serious accident. People get injured traveling the highways, working, and strolling the streets, yet no one suggests we stop these activities. We simply strive to perform them in a smarter, more aware fashion. This approach can also be applied with considerable success to paddling rivers.

Despite this, the potential for trouble always exists. Rapids are relentlessly powerful and totally uncaring. While often forgiving, they can be capricious and brutal, exacting a terrible price for mistakes. The dangers help us focus on the here and now while boating, not on the mistakes of the past or the uncertainties of the future. They teach us to be honest about our limits, to master our fears, and to work effectively under pressure. Great intelligence and integrity are required to gauge the risk and make the decisions needed to stay out of trouble time after time. Those who do are said to have good judgment; those who are always in trouble are courting disaster.

The paddlers who preceded me in the 50's and early 60's were true pioneers. Self-taught and analytical, many were scientists or engineers. They ran unknown rivers with homemade gear. Their guidebooks were highway road maps with thin blue lines for rivers. They were totally self-reliant. Although they traveled cautiously, they encountered plenty of trouble. Fortunately, the rapids they ran were easy by today's standards, providing an unexpected margin for error. And they learned a lot, leaving behind a few excellent books on technique and some well-written guidebooks for those who followed to build upon.

When I began paddling in the late 60's, whitewater paddlers were rare. You simply had to join a club to meet folks to run with! I was in college, so I started an outing club. We bought Grumman aluminum canoes. We read the AMC Whitewater Handbook. We bought used kayaks. The guys who had been lake canoeing before got to use the kayaks. We crashed and burned on local class II creeks, breaking boats and losing gear. We persevered. We taught ourselves how to roll from pictures in a book. We called the Penn State Outing Club, got some coaching, and learned how to build boats. We ran class III rivers that we'd never seen before, trembling with fear. We went to races and finished next to last. And we eventually got better.

Graduating in 1971, I plunged into the fascinating and obscure world of whitewater. If I saw someone else with a river kayak going the opposite way on an interstate, we'd both pull over and chat on the median. "What club are you with? Where do you paddle? Who has the mold for the latest hot boat?" We made better gear or bought it from someone in a club who sold it as a side business. We raced to improve our technique and boat control, then took these skills to the rivers. Here we astonished our elders by scouting class IV+ drops from our boats instead of from shore, a skill that opened up longer, more continuously difficult runs. We felt our way down classic runs like the Gauley, Chattooga, and Upper Yough in small groups. There were no crowds of rafts and paddlers to help us out if we ran into trouble, and this made us very, very cautious.

The sport grew rapidly over the next two decades. Soon you could buy a new kayak, take it to the river, and paddle it. You can now learn more about river running in a beginner kayaking clinic than we did in years of paddling with friends. Today everyone rolls. Some new paddlers work into hard rapids very quickly. Rivers are now very well known, and first-timers can be given very precise instructions on how to run a drop. New paddlers don't experience the low-intensity mishaps that we did, so when problems do arise, they have little knowledge to fall back on. Specialized river-rescue classes seek to fill that gap, with partial success.

The durability of plastic kayaks and canoes and the effectiveness of self-bailing rafts have opened up increasingly challenging runs, many with an absolutely unbelievable vertical component. These runs are the province of athletes as skilled and well conditioned as any member of the U.S. Whitewater Team. To make a name for himself or herself, a paddler must take serious risks. Many, many times my friends thought that a mistake would mean certain death, only to see the errant paddler flushed through some "unsurvivable" hole or chute. Paddlers now read the water better than we did, and they are better able to gauge the consequences of a miscue.

My primary goal has always been to avoid accidents, not deal with them. I started writing about fatalities and near-misses in the early 70's so that paddlers could learn from them. And we have. We no longer suffer the conceit that a trained, well-equipped paddler will never get into trouble. Foot entrapment, vertical pinning, and flush drowning—unknown when I started boating—have now been described. We know a lot more about boat outfitting, rope handling, and swimming than we did even ten years ago. But we have also seen that there is a random element of risk involved; some people don't make clear errors but die because they are unlucky. One of William Nealy's characters observed in his classic *Kayak* that it's usually better to be lucky than good, but I feel that luck always favors the prepared paddler.

These reports are the legacy of those who have died, or nearly died, on the water. Read them to avoid their mistakes. Remind yourself of the risks when scouting a rapid; the more dangerous the situation, the more sure you must be of success. And remember that the sport is supposed to be uplifting and fun; if it is not, something is wrong! If you are unfortunate enough to have a mishap, write it up and share it with others. Send reports to me at 230 Penllyn Pike, Penllyn, PA 19422, or call 215/646-0157.

See you on the river,
Charlie Walbridge

I was running sweep on a twelve-raft trip on the Nantahala River, just outside the Great Smoky Mountains National Park, when I rounded the corner above the beach at the top of the last drop on the section. Boaters often run the rapid, a class III called Nantahala Falls or Lesser Wesser, without scouting, but the raft trips pull in so that the customers can take a look at what they're getting into. The rapid is straightforward, with a left-to-right move required to avoid the grabby hole upstream on the right and a ledge hole on the bottom left. Although it is not a large rapid, the approach is long, wavy, and very fast, and the holes and cold water make for unpleasant swims. The hardest drop on this section of the Nantahala, the rapid is plenty challenging for the thousands of beginners and intermediate boaters who run it each season.

When I pulled in above the rapid, the other guides were heading the customers back upstream to the beach. The trip leader called me aside and told me that someone was trapped underwater below the ledge on the left. The accident scene, a popular boating spot near the Nantahala Outdoor Center, was covered with trained rescuers and there was nothing we could do to help. So we waited, along with guides from other trips, rafting customers, and many private boaters.

Eventually the victim was released, but too late (the account appears in Chapter 2), and the accident scene was cleared for river traffic. No obstruction had been found. No obvious, new dangers were reported.

I ran first. All the way down to the drop I talked to myself: "Take it easy. This is Lesser Wesser, class III, for God's sake. Just stay on line. Don't swim these folks."

Another voice in my head said over and over, "A man died here thirty minutes ago."

My run was fine. I eddied out below to set a rope for the following rafts, and a boater on the bank accosted me. "Don't you know someone just died here?" she asked heatedly. "Yes," I said. "I do."

My first experience with whitewater came in 1980 when some coworkers hired a local outfitter to take us on a raft trip down Section Nine of the French Broad River near Hot Springs, North Carolina. The sandwiches were soggy, we acquired a tear about two feet long in the floor of our raft, which we somewhat fixed with duct tape, and one of my friends got sunburned so badly that his arms and legs were covered with blisters for days. I was a teenager in love with the outdoors, and I decided after this one trip that river running was the life for me. More than fifteen years and literally thousands of days on rivers later, I still feel the same.

I have spent more time on the water as a raft guide than in any other way, primarily on the Chattooga, a beautiful and powerful river that runs between Georgia and South Carolina. But as a boater I have seen a fair sampling of what river running offers, from steep creeks to extended self-contained canoe camping trips, and I know both the rewards and the risks.

Many other books discuss the rewards—the why's, the where's, the how-to's. This book highlights the risks.

In Chapter 1 we discuss the type of boaters primarily described in this book, the nature and degree of risk involved in whitewater, and the need to group particular accident reports so that comparisons can be made. We also present the first three accounts, which show that some accidents provide clear lessons and some don't.

In Chapter 2 we present several accounts of fatal accidents that involve either inexperienced paddlers or paddlers with some experience on easy trips. The accounts vary from those showing gross errors to others where reasonable actions turn out badly.

Accidents recounted in Chapter 3 involve paddlers with considerable or great experience and skill, and the whitewater involved is generally more difficult than in earlier accounts. It is arguable that all victims in this chapter make errors of judgment that lead to their accidents, although in some cases it is only hindsight that allows us to see these errors. In other accidents the errors are clear. Running big drops, boating alone, and committing to a run you perhaps shouldn't be on are among the personal decisions we consider. Charlie also makes some observations about the aftereffects of being involved in a failed rescue.

In Chapter 4 we present the reports of three accidents, all occurring on trips of only two solo boats. Two-person trips, beyond being very convenient, have both positive and negative aspects. They build rapport and trust between two boaters in ways larger trips can't, but they also limit rescue options to those a person can manage alone. Both the good and the bad of two-person trips show up in these accounts, two of which are told by the surviving paddler.

The fifth chapter may be the most unsettling of the book, for in it we recount numerous accidents that lack clear and easily avoided causes. While most of these accidents occur on serious whitewater, most are suffered by experienced and capable boaters. These accidents cover the spectrum of whitewater risk, from long swims and recirculation to broaches and vertical pins.

Chapter 6 stands in happy contrast to the rest of the book, for in this chapter the victims survive. Sometimes skill pulls them through and sometimes luck. Often they are saved by the heroic efforts of their paddling companions. Many of these accounts are told by the victims, providing a different view of the perilous situation and the rescue attempts.

I hope that this book gives readers new perspectives on paddling. May it be a springboard for thoughtful discussion and a useful learning tool.

If in working with the varied sources of these accounts we have let errors of fact or interpretation creep in, they did so despite our best efforts to avoid them. Please let us know.

We present this book with sincere sympathy to the friends and families of the victims whose final moments are recounted here.

Enjoy your time on the water,
Jody Tinsley

1

The accounts that follow are drawn from the River Safety Task Force Reports of the American Canoe Association, a collection of four volumes covering the years 1976 to 1991. Each volume spans several years and reports in chronological order fatal and near-fatal accidents on whitewater rivers throughout North America. The purpose of these books is to present and analyze river emergencies so that paddlers can better understand the hazards of their sport and can learn, from both good and bad examples, how to minimize risk and how best to attempt rescue. The Reports do not attempt to be all inclusive, since recent accidents all too often are nearly exactly like earlier ones and thus provide no new lessons to the paddling community.

The objective of these Reports is primarily to gather accident accounts; the editor does not normally investigate them. The accident reports are drawn from many sources, ranging from careful and competent first-hand narratives by river or rescue professionals to conflicting statements from a collection of witnesses, some of whom know little about whitewater or are too emotionally involved to give a dependable report. Some are also based on newspaper accounts that may be oversimplifications. Still, the four volumes are a remarkably informative and often chilling record of 113 fatal whitewater accidents and 64 near-misses.

This book is a collection of those accounts and might be called the best of the worst, or the worst of the worst, given the subject matter. Some show clear mistakes, both gross and seemingly minor, that all river runners should learn to avoid. Some show rescue techniques that should be pondered upon and evaluated, either because they have been proven to work in certain situations or because they have been proven not to. Some show that, even without recognizable mistakes and even with well-considered and energetic rescue attempts, people die on whitewater, and people will die on whitewater in the future. How we come to terms with this indisputable truth in part defines us as whitewater boaters.

Most of us probably wish that we could somehow deny our own connection with the reality of whitewater deaths. In fact, the chances are that a proficient, active boater—not someone who fearlessly performs first descents in some mysterious, far-flung mountains, but rather someone who lives in the suburbs and spends an occassional weekend running moderately serious whitewater with a bunch of old friends—this person may well be involved with a river death some time over the course of a ten-year paddling career. If you are a serious boater and this hasn't happened to you yet, the question really is, "When will it happen?"

But realizing that each of us will likely be involved with a whitewater fatality is only a step along the way toward what for many of us is a harder truth, that each of us may be a whitewater fatality. Read the next sentence aloud: "I could be the next whitewater death." Any reaction?

When we think about it, we boaters generally accept this truth without much hesitation. We would rather die on a river than on an interstate, or in a hospital bed; if we didn't, we wouldn't keep running rivers. But how often do we think about it?

What if the victim were not you, but your best paddling partner, your trusted river amigo, your soul brother or sister, the most skilled, confident, cautious, respected boater you have ever known? Try saying the above sentence out loud again, but this time substitute the name of your best friend. Any reaction now? Disbelief? Sorrow? Regret?

Think of a group of paddlers sitting around, maybe talking over the day's trip, grinning, eyes bright, callused hands moving in space, conjuring up surfs and enders, drops and boof moves, runs historical, theoretical, apocryphal, holding forth with timing and animation, skill and showmanship greater than any magician or mime. These are your paddling friends; you are among them. Now imagine one less there the next day. It is of such people that the following accounts mainly speak.

The feeling that river accidents always happen to someone else is natural and widespread, and there are many reasons put forth to explain why a victim died that are couched in the form of judgment. For example, we might hear, "He shouldn't have been on that river in the first place. He wasn't experienced enough." On the other hand, someone might say, "He was too experienced not to know better. He must have gotten complacent." Or, "She always pushed herself. I guess she just pushed too far." And in contrast, "She never really played much. No wonder she didn't have the skills when she really needed them."

"He should have worked harder on his roll."

"She always thought a bomb-proof roll would let her crash and burn through anything."

"He always waited for someone to tell him what to do."

"She would never listen to anyone."

While comments like these are often accurate descriptions of a boater's character and are sometimes material to finding a cause for a specific accident, they are also often a convenient means for us to separate ourselves from river mishaps, or even from the very possibility of an accident. We may be saying, in effect, "He was flawed. I, however, do not have that flaw. His fate will not be mine." And certainly some characteristics, such as recklessness, are to be avoided if one wants a long river career, and some qualities, such as a healthy respect for the power of water, are to be cultivated. But boaters with most of the right characteristics and few of the wrong still die.

Perhaps risk should be seen not just as an intellectual and physical challenge that can be met and eliminated methodically and with consummate control by wit and skill—it is this, but perhaps it is more. Perhaps, even if we do not wish to admit it, risk on whitewater is more like a game of chess, but like a game of chess where every once in a while, without discernible pattern or obvious warning, one familiar piece turns into something else, something unexpectedly dangerous with a surprising ability to checkmate.

As much as we might wish it, there is no common thread that runs through the following accounts of river fatalities. These accounts vary as much as rivers and river runners, and any strict attempt to categorize them is bound to suffer from the flaw of oversimplification. But sometimes oversimplification is necessary, or at least justifiable, because of a need to present trends and to illustrate patterns.

While it is all too easy to point at one factor, one flaw as the reason for an accident, there are numerous exceptions—so numerous, in fact, that the patterns which actually do exist may be overlooked. However, it is worthwhile to look for the common elements in boating fatalities for what they teach. And it is possible to do this, at least to a degree, because serious boating accidents, including those occurring in canoes and kayaks, must be reported to the U.S. Coast Guard (USCG).

Under the Boating Safety Act of 1971, all boating accidents must be reported by the state boating law administrator to the USCG on a form called the Boating Accident Report, or BAR. As the BAR is designed primarily for gathering details of powerboat mishaps, it is extremely awkward for reporting facts of interest to nonpowered boaters. Getting useful information depends on having trained accident investigators. Not surprisingly, the quality of these reports varies from excellent to horrible. In states like Pennsylvania, Maryland, California, and Ohio, which have strong watercraft departments, descriptions are generally quite complete; in states where investigations are done by local law enforcement officers without much boating experience, it is often difficult to find out what happened. Good quality or not, the information from the reports is fed into USCG computers to create the boating statistics, which are published annually. But, the actual forms, interviews, and other materials, all of which is invaluable in understanding whitewater accidents, are protected by the Privacy Act, and it is very difficult to gain access to them for study.

However, in late 1978, experts from the American Canoe Association, American Whitewater Affiliation, and the U. S. Canoe Association conducted a review of accidents and fatalities of 1977 for the Coast Guard as part of an ongoing evaluation of floatation use in open canoes. The study, the first of its kind, convinced the USCG to concentrate its efforts on education rather than on design standards, saving hundreds of lives as well as millions of dollars for canoe buyers. Unfortunately, lack of funding and time prevented these studies from being continued.

A little over ten years later, in 1988, Joan Maybee, a master's degree candidate at Ohio University, assisted by the safety chairman of the American

Canoe Association, gained access to these BAR reports for study. As a prerequisite for gaining access, the Coast Guard and the American Canoe Association officially sanctioned her efforts. Maybee and several assistants spent a week in Washington studying the reports involving canoes, kayaks, and rafts. As part of her agreement with the Coast Guard, steps were taken to protect the names and addresses of individual victims and survivors. She was able to study the years 1984 (canoes only), 1985, and 1986. Like the previous investigators, she was frustrated by the poor overall quality of the reports, which prevented her from using the data the way she planned. But her findings are certainly valuable enough to share with the boating public.

Canoeing

Year	1977	1984	1985	1986
Number of Accidents	95	68	74	75
Number of Fatalities	131	83	80	84

Significant Factors (percentage)

Involving Whitewater	24	22	27	32
Cold Water (under 50°)	48	40	23	21
Involving Dams	8	12	5	4
Involving Strainers	3	6	9	6
PFD Not Worn, Not Used	85	75	58	63
Unable to Swim	60	21	15	9
Involving Alcohol	26	22	19	15
Overloading	3	2	1	9
Unable to Determine	5	9	3	11

The first thing to be noted is that most accidents do not occur in whitewater, but rather on calm rivers and lakes. Although the use of life jackets (PFDs) is growing, most victims, including many nonswimmers, choose not to wear them. Probably more than fifty percent of the fatalities in this study could have been prevented if the victim had simply been wearing a life preserver. Other major factors include alcohol use and boating on cold water, both of which are probably significantly underreported. It is likely that more than seventy percent of all serious accidents could be prevented by eliminating these three elements. Other factors like dams, strainers, and high water, very important to whitewater enthusiasts, are less important in the overall context of paddle

Kayaking

Year	1985	1986
Number of Accidents	9	8
Number of Fatalities	11	8

Significant Factors (percentage)

Whitewater	44	50
Cold Water (under 50°)	33	25
PFD Not Worn	33	13

Information on other causes is limited due to very low numbers of accidents.

sports. Although the tables do not show it, Maybee also found that spring and summer are the peak periods for serious accidents, but the off-season is probably more risky, with more fatalities per participant.

While each accident is certainly regrettable, given paddling's huge base of participation the overall safety record of paddle sports is good. Surveys commissioned by *Canoe Magazine* showed that in the mid-1980's almost nineteen million people participated in paddle sport activities each year, paddling ranking between tennis and downhill skiing in popularity, and the sport continues to grow. Although serious river runners are a definite minority, that's still a lot of people floating around. With so many people and abilities out on the water, someone is bound to get hurt. The sport grew thirty-three percent from 1983 to 1987, again according to *Canoe Magazine* surveys, but the number of fatalities remained stable. In light of this fact, the approximately 130 fatalities that occur each year in canoes, kayaks, and rafts seem pretty reasonable.

However, specifics for many accidents are unavailable. There is a desperate need for the Coast Guard to upgrade the BAR to collect more information of use to nonpowered boaters, and for that information to be regularly reviewed. Obviously, there is also a need for a more current study to see if the observed trends continue and to check for new ones. Until a new study is done, individual paddlers and paddling groups must work to draw conclusions from reports such as those presented by the River Safety Task Force.

For example, we can descry another low-head dam drowning and be fairly certain that this incident shares—too often, unfortunately—similarities with other accidents of this type, such as a lack of experience or a failure to scout. The "engineered drowning machine," as some have called low-head dams, has struck again, and questions concerning the type of accident and how to prevent more drownings supersede questions about the specific case, with all due respect to the individual who drowns.

Similarly, but on the positive side of the ledger, we can applaud the large and still growing number of boaters who have taken the time and trouble, out of a sense of responsibility and mutual regard, to learn and periodically recertify themselves in the skill of cardiopulmonary resuscitation (CPR), which gives them a chance to revive a drowning victim. Even though the success rate for this technique in a wilderness setting is low, often shockingly so to those who first hear the statistics, being trained gives rescuers at least a chance that they would not have had otherwise. The trend toward boaters becoming trained in CPR is notable, and the pattern of aggressive and well-executed resuscitation efforts is encouraging. Accounts where this skill makes all the difference, for example, could be grouped.

For these reasons, and without intending to deindividualize the following stories or to demystify the experiences of the people who set out alone, as we all must, on that last profound trip (or of those who nearly do but have the departure date postponed by skill or luck or both), we present these records grouped. Among the factors considered in making selections were accident type, size of the paddling party, and skill level. Sometimes stylistic considerations, such as length and tone of the original reports, influenced the order of the selections as well. However, throughout this collection of accounts, an overriding and natural division suggests itself; there are those accounts where a specific and obvious lesson is to be learned and those where it is difficult to find obvious errors—either in terms of judgment, equipment, or technique—and therefore hard to learn a clear lesson.

Sometimes one critical skill, learned often as not with a group of paddling friends, most of whom believed that what they were learning would be unlikely to have an effect on them, tips the balance in favor of successful rescue. Sometimes one critical skill not learned tips the balance toward failure. In the complex and subtle world of whitewater rescue, such clear-cut lessons are fairly rare. But since they provide boaters with an immediate and clear lesson that may, if appreciated and remembered (another issue entirely), save their lives or the lives of their boating partners, they are immensely valuable. The following account from 1975, when whitewater boating began growing in popularity faster than the fundamentals of river safety could be spread, gives boaters such a clear message.

Gene Bernardin

On the morning of October 4, during practice runs held prior to the annual slalom races on Ouleout Creek below the East Sydney Dam in south central New York, Gene Bernardin, an Appalachian Club member rated by those who knew him as a competent intermediate boater, capsized in midcourse, failed to roll up, and caught his foot on a submerged boulder while swimming.

The portion of the Ouleout Creek where the race is held is small and fast moving, but quite shallow. When 250-300 cfs are released, the difficulty of the rapids is probably class I-II. About two hundred yards below the dam, the river narrows below a bridge, dropping over a one- to two-foot ledge and creating a wave two to three feet high. Over the years, many people have safely swum this drop. Perhaps during the floods associated with Hurricane Eloise, a portion of this ledge broke off, becoming lodged at its base. This rock was completely invisible when covered with water and was not obviously dangerous even when the river bed was totally dry.

Gene and his partner flipped about seventy-five yards upstream of this point. Drifting downstream, his partner kept her feet up and flushed through to the eddy below. Gene tried without success to stand up in the rocky riverbed. As he went over the class II drop under the bridge, his foot became lodged in the crevice. The current swept him over onto his back, pushing him underwater.

Several boaters who were standing on shore witnessed the accident, jumped into the water, and tried to pull him free. At one time rescuers had hold of a leg and an arm but had no idea which way to pull, since only a dim outline was visible at the surface. Although a great deal of muscle power was available, no one could gain footing in the swift current. Just as a rescuer began to pull, his feet would be swept out from under him. On the far shore, several paddlers threw ropes across the river, and others tried in vain to pull Gene to the surface using the ropes. By this time, the flow from the dam had been shut off and the water had dropped. The rescuers were finally able to recover the victim. Mouth-to-mouth resuscitation was begun as soon as Gene's head cleared the surface, and CPR was performed by local rescue squad personnel. Oxygen was administered, and the ambulance arrived within minutes of the accident, but efforts to revive him were not successful.[1]

This type of accident is not a freak. In fact, it is probably the most common killer of river runners, and it provides a clear lesson. All paddlers must be aware of the danger of catching an extremity beneath a submerged object and must act accordingly. Feet, in particular, should be held high. This fact is sometimes not stressed to all beginners, but it should be. Under no circumstances should a paddler try to stand up in a strong current. Even if you don't get pinned, twisted or broken ankles are not uncommon. If the water is much more than a foot deep, swim toward shore and stand up only after you reach an eddy.

Very often, however, emergencies on the river pivot neither upon one critical error nor upon lack of a specific rescue skill or piece of river rescue gear. The death of a friend in a relatively simple accident because of someone's forgetting a knife, for example, or not knowing how to set up a tag line would undoubtedly haunt a boater for a long time. Usually, however, accidents are the result of a series of small omissions or errors, probably unrecognizable as such at the time and likely to be hardly recognizable, if at all, even with the clear vision of hindsight. Often our attempts to reconstruct the events leading up to an accident and to review the rescue effort, so as to learn what we can from the sad occurrence, do bear fruit. But sometimes, like all the king's horses and all the king's men, we are hard pressed to put together anything, not even a reconstruction of the accident, that answers the basic question: why? The next two accounts illustrate this difficulty.

Allan Connelly

In early March 1986, on a cold, rainy day, a group of paddlers from Atlanta arrived at the Gauley River in West Virginia. Finding it running very high, they elected to run the lower stretch. The victim

---

[1]*This was the first documented fatality foot entrapment, and it received the widest possible publicity to educate the beginner and to remind experienced boaters of the dangers.*

and all other members of the party were paddling low-volume squirt boats. Although the victim, Allan Connelly, had not been paddling very long and was the weakest member of the group, the day went well until the accident. It was cold, and Allan was probably tired when the group entered an eddy, peeled out, and headed downstream. The site appeared safe, and no one saw what happened; Allan simply disappeared without a trace. After an extensive search, the group left and notified authorities. The next day, with the flow cut back at Summersville Dam, Allan's body was located by professional guides who had joined the search. He was still in his boat, with the spray skirt attached. Jim Snyder, pioneer squirtist and boat designer, examined the kayak and the site. His report, slightly edited here, answers questions concerning how the boat may have been pinned.

"The scratches on the hull of the boat reveal a great deal. As there is only one set of fresh scratches, I am confident that they are caused by the accident. Some start at the feet and proceed to the hip area on the left side, and there are also some scratches approximately two feet long under the right hip. All of these scratches are relatively shallow except for one area under the left hip, where eight to ten zigzag scratches about three inches long are slightly deeper. These zigzag scratches are what I base my scenario on.

"Apparently, the boat was wedged with a rock at each hip. I believe he entered a drain area between two rocks at least three feet beneath the surface. The first point of contact was under his feet, but the boat slid forward two feet and lodged, blocking the drain. His bow was downstream, with the boat very near level. At this point I believe he dropped his paddle and put his hands on the rocks. In this position he wiggled the boat forward and back three inches at least eight times, but this effected no progress. As the scratches were not very deep, and the boat was not cracked, I believe there was a large area of contact with the rocks, creating too much friction for the boat to slide free. After several fierce attempts, he apparently quit suddenly and drowned without attempting to release his spray skirt."

This situation is unusual because Allan was trapped in an area underwater where the current drains between two rocks. Normally, boats are pinned at an angle to the current, creating a visible disturbance to the flow; had this been the case, Allan's party would perhaps have been able to locate him and begin rescue efforts. Because he was blocking the drain, a tremendous amount of friction prevented him from freeing the boat. Allan spent considerable energy trying, but he could not escape. The coroner's report states that there were no bruises on the body, ruling out entrapment and leaving us to wonder why he did not pop his spray skirt and attempt to escape the boat when it would not shake free, or even before trying to move the boat. His decision to attempt to move the boat was probably sound, and probably something most boaters would try naturally. However, in this case, for reasons not fully understood, Allan did not have the opportunity to try a second plan.

An accident the year before on the Merced River in California also involves this natural and often correct action of working a boat free using one's hands.

Mark Allen

On May 2, 1985, a group of expert kayakers was running a series of class III rapids found at the end of the Giant Gap run on the North Fork of the American River. While the Giant Gap run is part of a group of more difficult stretches opened up in California during the last decade, containing numerous class V rapids, the section of river where the accident occurred was class III at best. The flow of 1200 cfs is considered moderately high, but the group had no problems through the difficult rapids.

The victim, Mark Allen, 25, was considered to be one of the best boaters in the state. He had been paddling for four years and had risen quickly to expert status, frequently winning hot-dog contests. Just returning from an extended boating trip to Peru, he was in superb shape, and having run Giant Gap numerous times, he was very familiar with it.

At the accident site, the main chute, which is quite straightforward, is to the right, but Mark was livening up his run in this easier section by boofing offset boulders, a technique recently developed at the time of the accident that allows extremely obstructed chutes to be run. Mark missed his line, and his boat glanced off the upstream rock and pitoned on the one downstream. According to witnesses, Mark was not initially concerned, his face wearing a bemused expression as he tried to work his way free. Unfortunately, as his bow broke loose of the downstream boulder, the boat shifted, and his kayak wrapped fully around the upstream rock, sinking quickly out of view. The site was quite inaccessible, and although one of the group managed to swim out to the rock, he could offer no real assistance. Without options, the group paddled out and notified authorities, who returned with a cataraft to set up a Telfer lower at the site. They were able to snag Mark's boat with weighted grappling hooks, but the body was not found until almost three weeks later.

Beyond the blanket admonition to be careful and to treat the river with respect, there are several points to consider here. The first is that Mark chose to be in the obstructed left-hand chute, rather than in the normal class II-III drop. Many experienced paddlers, especially on rivers with which they are very familiar, deliberately choose difficult routes through easy rapids to spice up a run. Often, however, these side drops are not taken seriously enough. Increased difficulty increases risk, particularly in side chutes, which often have not been thoroughly scouted. Also, boofing pourovers to paddle rapids that otherwise might pin a boat means that pinning is a likely consequence of a missed move. This technique to keep the bow from diving has spread widely and is indispensable for tight runs, but it carries with it some added risk. Further, paddlers must recognize that simple pins in a powerful current, though seemingly harmless, are potentially very dangerous. It may be safer for other paddlers to lend a hand than for the pinned boater to shake loose. However, it can be nearly impossible or very dangerous for other boaters to reach a pin site. The desire not to endanger others, coupled with the tendency most boaters have to avoid asking for or receiving help, makes shaking loose a common option and one that is frequently successful. Exiting the boat is another, especially with the larger cockpits on current boat designs, but swimming obstructed passages brings its own significant risks.

As the two preceding accounts illustrate, many questions involving whitewater do not have simple right or wrong answers but require a careful weighing of options, considering both advantages and risks. Even for boaters with years of river experience, expert skills, and good instincts, the right balance of options is frequently uncertain, and the reason for failure is sometimes unclear. The simple fact is that whitewater paddling is not without risks, even for experts.

2

Through your consideration of the accounts in this book, we hope that you find the lessons of clearly right and wrong actions on rivers—and there are some actions that are certainly one or the other—graphically illustrated and the area of uncertainty somewhat smaller. This chapter begins with accounts where clear errors of judgment are made by beginners, leading to unfortunate but nearly inevitable consequences. However, by the end of the chapter the paddlers' errors are not obvious; in fact, some boaters, despite lack of experience, try to do everything right.

Although paddlers do well to remember that it is generally unfair to judge people who are caught in dangerous and stressful situations from the relaxed and coldly logical environment of home, there are certain acts or patterns of behavior and action that conscientious members of paddle sports must condemn, if only because these actions further the too-common stereotype of paddlers as either crazed risk takers or ignorant yokels. For example, while education as to the risks involved in whitewater and the proper methods of boating in reasonable safety is without doubt preferable to regulation that closes rivers in a supposed effort to protect people from themselves, some paddlers simply refuse to be educated.

The following account is such a case—where even though sympathy for the victim and his friends and family is, of course, in order, the actions of his group must be condemned.

Unknown Rafter on the Chattooga

On August 27, 1989, an inexperienced group of nine rafters attempted section IV of the Chattooga River, which forms the border between western South Carolina and Georgia. One of the two rafts flipped in the upper hole of Corkscrew Rapid, spilling five paddlers into the water. All five washed into Crack-in-the-Rock Rapid just below; only four came out. The remaining eight rafters proceeded to the take-out, not knowing their friend was pinned underwater.

The Chattooga has several sections of whitewater ranging in difficulty from class II to class V. Section IV is the most difficult stretch of the river, with many class IV-V rapids and an intense quarter mile known as the Five Falls, with a gradient of more than 200 feet per mile. Crack-in-the-Rock, the site of the accident, is the third of the Five Falls. A level of 1.65 feet at the Highway 76 bridge, boosted by inflow from Stekoa Creek downstream, is considered moderate but not to be trifled with.

Nine healthy college men rented two rafts and equipment for eight at a local whitewater shop. The weekend rental came with the explicit agreement that the group was to raft sections II and III only and was by no means to go beyond the Highway 76 bridge. Instead, the group rafted sections III and IV. The ninth member, for whom no life jacket or helmet had been rented, went on the river instead of running shuttle.

Teresa Grider, local boater and raft guide, continues the narrative, with some input from Dennis Kerrigan:

"I saw the group on Saturday running Bull Sluice, the class IV+ finale to section III. It is not unusual to see rental rafts out of control in this drop, but this group was exceptional. Out of four men in the first raft, none had on helmets; only three were wearing life jackets, and none of these were zipped. They hit Decapitation Rock and nearly flipped, dumping the crew out. The fellow without a life jacket was under water long enough for me to wonder if he were trapped. They were drunk, and the smell of alcohol was strong. The second raft's run was unremarkable, with only a few swimmers. There were no rangers at the site, and the men were unresponsive to our advice when our group tried to talk with them. When asked about the missing life jacket, they claimed they had lost it upstream.

"On Sunday, August 27, eight men with all the required equipment put in at the 76 bridge. River Ranger Tina Barnes was on site. Knowing that rental gear is not supposed to run this stretch, she tried to talk the group out of going but could not detain them because no Forest Service regulations were being violated. They probably picked up their ninth, unequipped member downstream.

"Sometime around 2:00 P.M. the nine men made it to the Five Falls. One of the rafts flipped in the large pourover at the top of Corkscrew Rapid, just upstream of Crack-in-the-Rock. Five men floated past several eddies into Crack. One swam in the direction of Left Crack, where there have been two previous deaths, and disappeared. The rafter without the life jacket swam through Middle Crack, also a known death trap, and flushed through. The remaining three apparently went through Right Crack, which is less hazardous and is chosen by most paddlers. Boaters several rapids below knew there had been a mishap because of helmets and paddles being washed downstream, but there were no experienced boaters at the site to attempt a rescue. Shortly thereafter a pair of kayakers, after questioning the rafters, paddled out and notified the Forest Service that one person had disappeared while swimming Left Crack. The rest of the group, assuming that their buddy had hiked out, continued downstream to the take-out, where they remained until they got a shuttle with the coroner.

"Left Crack is about three feet wide and four feet high, with the water pillowing against the river-left side. There is a log, and perhaps a rock, that leans upstream deep in the powerful currents at the foot of the drop. The victim apparently swam into the crack feet first. His legs must have gone under the obstacle, as his body was folded over by the force of the water. He was still wearing his life jacket.

"River Ranger Buzz Williams was the first on the scene. He, along with Southeastern Expeditions and Nantahala Outdoor Center guides, located the body by poking around in the drop with a stick, and the extrication was begun. After a snag line failed, a raft was hauled into the drop from downstream, and two rescuers were able to attach a rope to the victim's waist. Three hours, six Z-drags, a come-along, and a vector pull later, the victim was freed. Twenty-five people had hiked or boated in by the time he was released. The rescue was well executed, with Buzz Williams (USFS), Dennis Kerrigan (NOC), and Andy Smith (SEE) providing the leadership. At about 6:30 P.M. the victim was placed in a body bag and rafted out.

"Although the victim was wearing a life jacket and apparently knew that in general in whitewater a swimmer needs to go down river feet first, the group did practically everything wrong. The members were unfamiliar with the river. They were improperly equipped. Their lack of skill put them in the water at a dangerous place, and they were fortunate that several fatalities did not result. It's hard to know what more could have been done to prevent this 'Deliverance Trip' from getting on the Chattooga. The outfitter renting to these men told them not to attempt this section of the river. Ranger Barnes did her best to persuade them not to go on section IV, both at 76 bridge and again downstream at Woodall Shoals. All this went unheeded."

This fatality was caused by ignorance on the part of the group combined with a bad attitude that prevented them from receiving advice about the river from experienced people. While it is true that only individual paddlers can decide if they are capable of a specific run, it is also true that ignoring the advice of outfitters, experienced boaters, and the authorities entrusted with protecting you, as well as the whitewater resource, defies logic. Everyone involved made his or her best effort to protect these people from themselves.

This accident is also a grim reminder of the difficulties of extracting a body from a severe pin and should make us all cautious in similar situations. Rescuers on the scene reported that the force required for twenty-five people using seven ropes to pull out the victim was phenomenal. One of the rescuers, Dennis Kerrigan later wrote, "I am convinced that there is no possible way to save somebody who washes into Left Crack at hazardous levels (1.4-1.8 feet).

The only protective safety measures are knowledge of the hazard and appropriate back-up measures to guard against a swim through Left Crack. In this particular drowning, virtually identical in mechanism to the previous two, these procedures were noticeably absent." Once the victim lodged in Left Crack, the result was inevitable.

Although not as long as the preceding account, and certainly not played out by people so obviously disregarding good advice, the two following actions show a similar disregard for the fundamentals of river safety or perhaps a lack of knowledge which proved fatal. Sometimes the dividing line between ignorance and poor judgment, between lack of experience and carelessness, is hard to draw. But in a sport where none of these flaws is required for accidents to strike, any one of them is more than sufficient.

Nonswimmer on the Delaware River

On a spring day in 1990, a party of five rented a raft for a day of paddling on the upper Delaware River, near Port Jervis, New York. They received the usual safety lecture from Kittatiny Canoes, which is quite adequate, and set out.

The party had just come through the class II rapid created by the confluence with the Mongaup River. Wary of the rapids, the victim had been wearing his PFD, but he removed it shortly after they made the run. While floating through a calm stretch with a moderate current, the victim and another member of the party began to roughhouse. Both individuals, neither wearing a PFD, fell into the water at about 2:50 P.M. This section of river is about fifteen feet deep, and the victim was unable to swim. A PFD was thrown to the victim; he surfaced two or three times but could not grab it. Members of his party and kayakers who were nearby made an effort to rescue him, but without success. The body was not recovered until 4:30 P.M., after divers from the Port Jervis Dive Team arrived.

Everything possible was done to help the victim, from the time his party had rented the raft to the actual rescue. The outfitter had provided adequate safety instruction and gear. But instruction will not help those who do not follow it, and life vests won't work if they aren't worn.

The next record tells of the deaths of three members of the same family, the entire boating party. Since there were no survivors and no witnesses, details are few. But it is clear that the party made at least one fatal mistake— running, intentionally or not, a low-head dam.

Reggie, Ronald, and Stacy Tate

In late May, tragedy struck on one of the most popular canoeing streams near Eagle Grove, Iowa. Two brothers and a nephew drowned when their canoe went over Corn Belt Power Dam at Humboldt on the Des Moines River.

The three launched their canoe above the dam at 9:30 A.M., intending to go down eight miles or so to near Badger, where they had left a pickup truck. A search of the river began late in the day when their overturned canoe was sighted and pulled ashore fifteen miles downstream near Ft. Dodge.

Reggie's body, wearing a life jacket, was recovered 200 yards below the dam about 8:00 P.M. The bodies of Stacy and Ronald were located several days later.

Reggie was an instructor at University of Northern Iowa and was studying for his Ph.D. Ronald was a farmer who left a wife and two daughters. Stacy, a four-year honor student in high school, was to enter Iowa State in the fall.

The dam is only three feet high.

Before we judge these people too mercilessly, saying they only got what they deserved, let us remember the times when, for whatever reason, we haven't gotten what was coming to us. Let us each be thankful that our own errors of judgment and bullheadedness have so far led us only into near catastrophe.

There are many people who have gotten much more than they deserved, who, because of occasional minor lapses of judgment, or over-estimates of skill, or more commonly, nothing more serious than bad luck, have been charged the ultimate price for their pains. If some paddlers want to cling to the idea that those who are hurt or killed on rivers somehow deserve to be in cosmic payback for pride, carelessness, some lack of skill, or a bad attitude, believing that careful people, staying reasonably safe, using proper gear and paddling within their skill level, will stay out of trouble, these accounts may shake their faith. We can shrug off many stories of fatalities because the victims are not like us, not doing the things we do on whitewater. Maybe they are novices, doing everything wrong, unwilling to learn the right way. Maybe they are running rivers or making individual moves of extreme difficulty, being dare-devils, as some might say. But the following accounts resist being shrugged off easily. They are tenacious. They cling. Beginners, with good intentions and attitudes, trusting the experts, trying their best to learn correctly, and experienced folks enjoying mellow trips well within their level of skill, frequently with extensive experience, at home on the water, die also.

Larry Barkdale

As many paddlers would, Larry Barkdale and his wife decided to enjoy some vacation time in late summer by taking an eight-day canoe trip. Their choice was the Middle Fork of the Salmon River in Idaho. The Middle Fork is a large-volume whitewater stream that is extremely popular for overnight float trips. Larry Barkdale, 48, a former professional guide, was paddling with his wife in a tandem canoe. On this, the last day of their trip, they had successfully run Weber Rapid and were navigating its swift runout when their boat suddenly flipped in the currents below. As they were swimming their boat to shore, Larry became trapped against a large rock with a crevice in it, which formed a deadly strainer. He cried out for help and then was forced underwater. By the time other members of his party had assembled with ropes to offer assistance, it was too late. After working for more than an hour to release Larry, the group sent for help. Forest Service personnel came back later and recovered the body.

Except for flipping, which is part of the tandem experience, the victim and his party made no errors that might have led to this accident. No other guides on the river knew about this particularly dangerous spot. The only moral is that many well-known rivers harbor treacherous places that are neither well known nor marked. Extra care in avoiding unfamiliar places, particularly when out of the boat, is always well advised, but most competent boaters are, of course, careful whenever they swim. Larry just found himself in the wrong place.

Sherry Lee Gilbert

In another canoeing accident, a 24-year-old woman drowned when her canoe capsized on the Machias River, near Ellsworth, Maine, pinning her legs under the seat as the force of the water bent the canoe in half. Warden Neal Wykes of the Maine Department of Inland Fisheries and Wildlife said that the victim, Sherry Lee Gilbert, was kneeling in the bow of the canoe when the accident occurred at the foot of Carrot Pitch Rapid.

Sherry was one of six women who set out one Sunday morning in June 1989 on what was to be a six-day canoe trip from First Machias Lake to Whitneyville. When the canoeists reached Carrot Pitch, four of the women elected to portage the rapid because of high water. Sherry and a friend, Karen Marysdaughter, who had run the rapid on a previous trip, decided to make the run.

They were almost through when they got out of the channel they were in and hit a rock. This turned the canoe sideways and flipped it upstream, filling it with water and bending it around the rock. Sherry's legs were caught between the floor of the canoe, which buckled, and a thwart, and the force of the water shoved her under the canoe. She apparently never broke the surface after the pinning.

Wykes said that Karen tried to free Sherry but was swept away by the current. Another woman attempted to get to the canoe from shore, but the power of the water would not let her near it. Two of the women left for help and were picked up by fishermen. Wykes, along with Wardens Philip White, David Craven, and Michael Marshall, responded to the call. The four men took forty-five minutes to break the thwart and extricate Sherry, but the canoe was wrapped so tightly around the rock that they were forced to leave it until the water level dropped.

Wykes said that Sherry's was a freak accident, because most people are thrown out of a canoe when it capsizes in rapids. While this is true, additional floatation inside the open canoe could have made the pin less severe and perhaps made rescue possible. Frequently, though, floatation in an open canoe is removed before a multiday trip to provide room for camping gear. This practice is reasonable in most cases, but it does add risk. Generally, however, the consequences for a mistake are limited to a swim and some damp gear for the rest of the trip. A broach is possible, but a broach where someone is pinned in an open canoe is indeed rare. Unfortunately for Sherry, hers was the rare case.

Ian Jenkinson

In 1990, Ian Jenkinson was also the unfortunate, rare exception when he and his partner flipped their canoe about thirty feet above the final drop of Nantahala Falls. The Nantahala River upstream of the Nantahala Outdoor Center, near Wesser, North Carolina, is one of the East's busiest rivers, and thousands of people have swum Nantahala Falls without problems. The victim, a tandem boater from Great Britain, was paddling with a group when he capsized. Both paddlers swam through the Nantahala Falls in the correct swimmer's position: on their backs with feet up. While his partner floated straight through the rapid, Ian vanished in the bottom hole left of center. A few moments later, his helmet and life jacket washed out, a sure sign of desperate trouble.

Although this was not a commercial trip, a number of NOC staff members were on the scene within minutes. A rope was strung across the river, and Kurt Doettger waded out, using the rope, to try to locate the victim, who was nowhere in sight.

Suddenly Doettger's foot became entrapped, probably in the same spot where Ian had disappeared. After exhausting himself in an attempt to remain upright on the rope, he let go and disappeared. After a brief time, he floated up, face down, with his life vest up over his head and elbows. Doettger came to as he was pulled from the water; he has no memory of going under but believes his foot was caught when the straps of his river sandals became hung on a rock. He suffered minor injuries to his foot, ankle, and knee and was treated and released at a local hospital.

Local rescue squads responded about forty-five minutes after the accident, and soon after, NOC staff member Kory Kais caught sight of Ian's hand floating near the surface. After tying the rope to his wrist, rescuers were able to pull him out upstream. CPR was begun immediately, and the victim was transported to a hospital, where he was pronounced dead. Ian's legs were badly bruised from the knees down; it was apparently a full foot and lower leg entrapment.

John Burton, in the NOC staff newsletter, writes, "Hundreds, perhaps thousands of paddlers have swum through the very spot where Ian became entrapped. Our best guess is that the March floods may have scoured some of the smaller rocks from the base of the ledge, exposing several small crevices and pockets into which a foot would fit. At dawn the following day, staff from at least three river companies gathered to inspect the Falls with the water turned off. The group found a number of small possible entrapment spots which were filled with rocks of various sizes until the consensus was that the danger of a repeat problem at this spot was considerably reduced. Continued monitoring of the area, especially after major floods, will help insure against further trouble."

While these efforts are commendable, Ian Jenkinson will reap no benefits from them. Again, unless someone wishes to argue that flipping a tandem canoe in a class III-III+ rapid is a grave error, the price he paid seems out of proportion to his mistakes. His death, however, has added support to the idea that the traditional feet-first swimming position is not the best choice for steep drops, where vertically pinning the feet is a real concern. Bending the legs or even curling into a ball on these drops lessens this risk.

It is also worthwhile to note the entrapment possibilities of river sandals both in and out of the boat. As comfortable and as popular as these sandals are, booties or even sneakers may reduce entrapment risk.

Entanglement of many kinds is a real possibility since river running inevitably involves ropes and straps of various sorts. An incident on the Salmon River near Pulaski, New York, illustrates this danger, but the entanglement, as far as can be determined from the account, is not due to mishandled or poorly attached gear. If attributable to anything, the entanglement is the result of an inability to recognize a serious danger spot. This characteristic, of course, describes many if not most beginner trips.

Dean Middleditch

On Sunday, March 19, 1990, five kayakers met to run New York's Salmon River, a popular class II-III novice run that was bank-full thanks to recent rains and snowmelt. The victim, Dean Middleditch,

25, had done some kayaking in England but had never been in fast-moving water.

The group ran the river once, taking out at Black Hole. On this first trip, they ran to the right of a large island, avoiding the site of the accident. On their second, shorter run from the Fairgrounds down, they chose the other channel. Here the right bank is badly eroded and the exposed tree roots have snagged considerable debris. It is a known danger spot; several years previously a Boy Scout overturned his canoe at this spot and was rescued by a local kayaker who lives near the river.

On the second run, Middleditch was the last to enter the channel. He flipped, failed to roll, and exited. Swimming with his boat, he was swept under a tree, where he disappeared and never came up. Since the rapid is in the town of Pulaski, rescue personnel were summoned quickly. Niagara Mohawk turned off an upstream dam, and two hours later the water began to recede. Dean's body was recovered several hours later; his life vest had apparently snagged on a branch.

It is clear that this group did not exhibit the best possible judgment that day. March 19 is late winter in northwest New York, and cold weather and high water are extreme conditions for a first whitewater run. Middleditch would have been well advised to wait for better weather and water, and the group should have considered staying away from the fatal channel, which has little to recommend it. But many a boater has made a similar run [maybe several, early in his or her whitewater career]. We have frozen our tails off on no-name little creeks and eddied out behind trees once we were committed for the first time to a high-water fiasco. And we've laughed about it later. Dean Middleditch was no more guilty of gross errors in judgment than most of us have been from time to time.

Unfortunately, even beginners who recognize their own lack of experience and choose to take guided trips cannot count on finding the safety they seek, even when the guides are faultless.

Jack

For one client, a guided trip on the Rio Jatate in Mexico during the winter of 1986 turned out to be the last adventure. This river

'We have frozen
on no-name creeks
and eddied out behind
trees once committed for the
first time to a high
water fiasco.'

flows through a steep-walled tropical gorge of remarkable beauty south to the Guatemalan border and has become a popular self-supported kayak trip. This particular run was organized by Slickrock Kayaks and included participants with a wide range of abilities. Each boat was weighed down with food and personal gear, but this proved not to be a factor in the accident or ensuing rescue attempts.

In the middle of the first rapid, one member of the trip, identified only as Jack, hit an undercut midstream boulder. Although warned to avoid the rock, he did not, nor did he respond well to the collision, flipping violently upstream and pinning fast. Trip leader Erdman, in position with a throw line, swam out to the rock and released the kayak within seconds. He saw no sign of Jack, who was evidently trapped near the base of the boulder.

Erdman lost his footing and had to swim downstream. As he floated away, Bob McDougal got himself into position above the rock. Taking unusual risks, he was able to grab Jack's arm. Less than a minute had elapsed, and Jack, if he had been released, would have had excellent chances of recovery, but Bob could not pull Jack free. A rope was tied to Jack's arm, and the group pulled on him from downstream, but without success. Then rope was attached to his torso; it frayed and snapped, a token of the time and energy spent in the rescue attempt. By now it was clear that Jack was beyond help, and the group made camp in the fading tropical light. A line was left tied to Jack's hand to facilitate extrication the next day. Tied to the rescue line, which could not rescue, Jack's body waited for removal.

In the morning, it took more than an hour to release the body, which was then wrapped in a sleeping bag and placed inside a kayak. It was hauled to a trail on the canyon rim and returned to developed areas on horseback.

It is clear from the description that the group performed well during the rescue and the evacuation. Given the water's force in this entrapment, once Jack pinned against that rock, he was as good as dead. It is also clear from remarks that Jack had made to the group that he lacked the skills needed for remote expeditioning on intermediate whitewater. He was one of the weakest boaters of the group and was clearly uncomfortable with what he was doing. He was overweight, asthmatic, and in generally poor physical shape; one has to wonder why he chose to go on this trip, exotic and beautiful though it was. He did not have the experience needed to follow the guide's instructions to get through a difficult drop. Perhaps, despite his lack of ability and his physical problems, he believed by putting himself in the hands of a reputable outfitter that he had sidestepped the risks, that he would be okay. However, the strengths and pitfalls of guided river trips are highlighted here: clear instruction and a fast and competent rescue are no guarantee of safety for someone lacking the fundamental boating skills required to stay out of trouble. Paddlers signing up for these activities must take care to be as honest as possible about their skills and to find out as much as they can about the river, since only they can tell if the risks are appropriate for them.

Screening applicants for trips is difficult over the phone, and Jack's apparent opinion that the skills of the outfitter would outweigh his own shortcomings is a commonly held view. Indeed, most of the millions who go on commercial rafting trips hold this opinion, and it generally proves true. But the requirements placed on a member of a team on an extended wilderness kayak trip are greater than those placed on nearly all rafters, and the outfitter's ability to protect is proportionally less. Evidently Jack did not understand this central point.

On the other hand, neither a misrepresentation of skill level by a novice nor a misunderstanding of what he was getting into can be blamed for the death in the following account. Roger Stallings played every card correctly—in fact perfectly—when he signed up for a kayaking clinic taught by the Nantahala Outdoor Center, an organization with a worldwide reputation for whitewater instruction. He still lost his life in a bizarre, unprecedented boating accident.

Roger Stallings

Roger Stallings, 30, of Greenville, Tennessee, drowned while paddling a kayak on the Tuckasegee River near Dillsboro, North Carolina, on July 9, 1989. The kayak clinic put in below the dam at Dillsboro and moved down the river about a mile and a half. A hundred yards below the Railroad Bridge Rapid (class II), a small island splits the river, narrowing it to a channel perhaps seventy feet wide with a fast chute of current and several standing waves about a foot high. The last wave breaks back to form a small hole. On the river right of the chute is a large rock some four feet in diameter that sticks out of the water about three feet. Below this rapid—it is stretching things slightly to call it class II—is a deep pool, and then the river broadens and becomes very shallow.

The lead instructor took two students with him to run down through this rapid, and the rest of the students were to follow him single file through the wave train. The assistant instructor stayed above to assist the remaining members of the group. Stallings was the next to last to run. At the bottom, his boat stopped abruptly in the middle of the wave and then folded, with the stern climbing into the air. In less than a minute, according to witnesses, the stern folded over, forcing his head underwater.

Roger pinned, as later investigation would show, on an industrial conveyer belt lodged underneath the rock on the right. The belt looped out into the current more than halfway across the chute and was hidden in the wave hole at the bottom. The belt was some 18 inches wide and made of an extremely stiff rubberized material. Its length is unknown, since efforts to remove it were not entirely successful. Facing edge-on to the current, the belt moved dynamically and randomly up and down. There was no surface signature of this deadly snare. Only a half hour before, another kayak clinic had run this same rapid with no problems. However, the bow of Roger's kayak, a Perception Dancer, evidently became caught in a loop of the belt. Clearly it was a matter of timing; Roger's bow plunged down into the wave at the same time the belt surged up.

The two instructors began rescue efforts immediately, but it was nearly ten minutes before they were able, at considerable risk to themselves, to attach a rope to the boat's grab loop and begin to pull it free. During the rescue, Roger's body washed out of the boat, disappearing downstream. It was not recovered until several days later.

This is the type of accident that haunts every kayak instructor and every river runner. The hazard was invisible, unexpected, and deadly. In fact, the instructors did not know until the next day, after an investigation by rescue squad members, exactly what had caused the pinning. A local outfitter claims to have seen the belt upstream and to have tried to remove it during an earlier river cleanup trip. In his opinion, the belt moved downstream during the high water the week before the accident. Since the Tuckasegee flows through several small towns and has some industry on its banks and tributaries, there is a fair amount of junk in the river, although most of it is harmless. Certainly it is irresponsible, although unfortunately not unusual, to throw things like conveyer belts in the river, but given that such hazards exist, what can we learn except, obviously, to avoid them if possible? What more could Roger or the instructors have done to be safer? If one decided to run only those rivers completely free of man-made debris, then new difficulties and dangers would appear due to remoteness.

Rescue efforts by the instructors were quick and effective, but a situation like this simply points up the lack of time in a head-down pin. Rescuers have only three to five minutes at most to assess the situation and extricate the victim. The only possible criticism of the rescue is that both instructors exposed themselves to a great deal of danger in their attempts to rescue Roger Stallings.

The boat folded just forward of the cockpit, but the craft is not to blame. It appears from examining the boat that a loop of the belt slid up the left side of the boat until it was stopped by the cockpit. A European bulkhead design would have most likely folded even sooner, because the belt pressed against the unsupported side of the boat rather than the bow. A fiberglass boat with a breakaway cockpit might have broken enough to let the paddler get free, although this is by no means certain. In short, the vertical wall system favored in this country worked as well as anything could have been expected to.

Everything was great that day on the Tuckasegee. A man was learning to kayak the right way, in an easy, well-known river, under good instruction. New friends were sharing anticipations, excitement, laughter. The summer sun in a blue sky peered down on green mountains. A whole new world of river sport was opening. Waves beckoned. The man's turn came. And then it was over. Everything was great that day until Roger Stallings died.

3

In the preceding account, Roger Stallings died although he chose a careful and prudent approach to learning about whitewater. In contrast, some people, like the rafters on section IV of the Chattooga whose accident is recounted earlier in this book, err clearly on the side of recklessness. The reasons vary: a need to prove themselves, a desire to achieve an impressive reputation in boating circles, a failure to understand the power and dangers of rivers, an overinflated self-confidence and a sense of invulnerability, faith in the sincere belief that absolutely nothing is impossible to the dedicated, well-trained boater, or maybe something else entirely. Boaters wager all they have on their judgment, sometimes on one quick throw of the dice. In the accounts that follow, three people lose their bets.

In 1988, on January 1, a day that traditionally symbolizes new beginnings, Ray Wiseman, 27, a three-year raft guide and first-year kayaker with excellent skills, died after attempting a run of Eagle Falls on the South Fork of the Skykomish River, in Washington State.

Ray Wiseman

Eagle Falls, rated class VI by locals, is a nasty drop. Ray Wiseman was evidently off his line when he spun into a large boulder at the lip of the Falls. Dropping over backwards, his boat caught on a rock midway down the Falls and pinned there for between six and fifteen minutes. Eventually, the boat released itself with the boater still inside, and the body was recovered by his companions. CPR was begun by a Seattle firefighter who saw the accident while driving by. Basic life support continued for thirty minutes, until paramedics arrived. In their care, Ray was intubated and transferred by ambulance to life flight in critical condition. Despite the efforts of trained personnel, giving quick and effective life support at the accident site, and excellent continuing care, Ray never recovered. He was declared brain dead three days later.

While we can learn from this accident that errors in boat control have serious consequences on drops of this magnitude, we cannot learn what motivated Ray Wiseman to attempt the drop in the first place. And what significance, if any, does the choice of New Year's Day have? Many boaters had an opportunity to contemplate this question, as this accident, captured on videotape and sold to CNN, was seen by paddlers throughout the country.

Especially in serious whitewater, death may be a single paddle stroke away, and those who seek extreme challenge must never underestimate the risk. Ray's run went horribly wrong, but it is ironic to consider that if he had been successful, his run might have contributed to an accident at this site. A successful run often encourages others to follow, frequently those who are less skilled. Any difficult rapid that is run cleanly looks easy, but looks are deceiving, a point we all need to keep in mind. Still, most paddlers—some would say the conscientious ones—understand that their choices and actions have a powerful effect on less experienced boaters and that the publicity their actions generate affects the public's perception of paddle sports. But boaters are an independent lot, and some naturally chafe at this responsibility, maintaining that one person's actions are wholly separate from another's and that the overall image of paddle sports is none of their concern.

Lack of concern might well summarize the next account, where an experienced kayaker drowned below a dam on a class II run in New Jersey.

Ken Kajiwara

The Pequannock River through Pompton Plains creates, at high water, a passable after-work run for local paddlers. The good news is that the rapids are not difficult and have nice waves and strong eddies. The bad news is that the four or five dams on this short run have to be portaged, breaking up the continuity of the run, and the steep concrete-lined banks make access difficult in many places.

The victim, Ken Kajiwara, was part of a group of locals making the run on May 17, 1989. He was an experienced boater familiar with the run, described by his friends as a very go-for-it person with the nickname Kamikaze Ken. The others in the group were equally competent but more conservative in temperament.

On arriving at the first dam, the group portaged. Ken, however, felt that the dam could have been run, and he berated his buddies for sucking him into the carry. At the second dam, the group pulled over into an upstream eddy formed by the pumping station. Ignoring their warnings, Ken paddled right on past. He hit the hydraulic upright and was immediately flipped. Bailing out, he was caught in the hydraulic's maw, far out of the reach of throw bags. His horrified companions could only watch as he was recirculated for fifteen minutes. Finally he was kicked out, only to float over two more dams before being pulled from the river by nonboaters. At this point, he still had a heartbeat and was taken to a hospital by rescue squad members, but Ken died the following day.

Despite whatever reasons he may have had, this run showed an appalling lack of judgment on the part of the victim. Dams are known to be dangerous. We all know they sometimes don't look bad, but their currents form a deadly trap, as the accident in the previous chapter involving members of the Tate family makes horribly clear. We can tell of this danger over and over, trying to be sure that everyone gets the message, but a number of trained whitewater boaters seem unwilling to listen. Although expert boaters can safely run some dams at appropriate water levels, scouting and setting safety personnel downstream are called for. Had Ken placed boaters below the drop, he might have been rescued, and this precaution, plus scouting, would have made his run a calculated risk, even though the huge, powerful hydraulic would certainly have posed a grave danger to rescuers. As it was, he didn't bother. Unfortunately, Ken's run is exactly the kind of irresponsible activity that gives paddlers a bad name and leads to the closure of excellent places for whitewater sport in heavily populated areas.

Ken's friends were not influenced by his run other than to have their already displayed desire to stay away from dams reinforced. A rescue technique that might have been tried in this situation involves tying a rope, or several ropes tied together, to a kayak. The kayak is then intentionally surfed into the hydraulic in hopes that it will move along the hole to the location of the victim while pulling the safety rope farther than it could be thrown. This technique has been practiced by some rescue groups, but there have been no saves reported yet. Still, the point is that Ken should not have been in the hole to start with.

Many would say that Jesse Sharp, 28, should never have been where he was, either—in a C-1 running Niagara Falls.

Jesse Sharp

Sharp arrived in Buffalo, New York, in June 1990, with the clear intention of running the Falls. A highly skilled paddler who lived in a tent along the banks of the Ocoee River in Tennessee during the summer, he had trained by running various falls in the Smoky Mountains and felt he was ready; to record his descent on video, he brought several friends along. Niagara Falls needs little introduction. It's 181 feet high, a full hundred feet higher than the highest successful falls run on record at that time. The river flows at 250,000 cfs, and its huge volume adds to the difficulty. While it is clearly unrunnable in the recognized sense of the word, people have survived the plunge in barrels, and in one instance, in only a life vest.

But running the Falls had apparently been Jesse's life's ambition. He had told many paddlers of his goal and had tried ten years earlier, but he was stopped then when his parents tipped off police. This time he planned not only to run the Falls but also to navigate the whirlpool and rapids below. These rapids themselves are very serious business, run only by teams of experts, and inexplicably Jesse wore no life vest or helmet during his attempt. After making plans to meet friends at a boat ramp in Lewiston, New York, and then to have dinner, he launched. Bare-chested in the huge water above the drop, he twirled his paddle confidently at the lip of the Falls, a signal to his friends that he was on his line. One has to imagine the thrill of the big waves and the view opening up below him as he approached his final horizon line.

Immediately after, his run fell apart. His bow was tucked under by the falling water, and he started to tumble. Those who have seen his boat believe that he hit rocks at the base of the falls. Hundreds of tourists on both sides of the river witnessed his plunge, and the video made the evening news throughout the country.

While advances in boating during the past decades have made most pad-dlers unwilling to say that something cannot be run, let's make an exception here. It seems clear that someone of Jesse's experience should have developed a better appreciation for the nature of his undertaking. However, his friends, when interviewed by the police, did not agree, saying, "Until someone's tried it, you don't know it can't be done." It is true that boaters are running rapids considered impossible a decade ago, but progress has come in carefully rea-soned steps. Some people take larger steps than others, but knowledge and skill, not blind courage, are the basis for their success.

The whitewater community has long championed the right of boaters to take calculated risks in pursuit of their sport, and most paddlers feel that people should be allowed to try any damn-fool stretch of river they care to as long as no one else is endangered. But this fiasco went beyond the rules of ordinary risk-taking; it was on par with playing Russian roulette with a fully loaded weapon and hoping for a misfire. Sure, Jesse might have made it. A little girl wearing only a life jacket survived being swept over the Falls after a canoe she was paddling with her father capsized upstream. Her father, not wearing a life vest, perished, making Jesse's refusal to wear protective gear that much harder to understand. But questions of equipment and even skill are moot in the face of this undertaking. If Jesse had survived, it would have been due simply to miraculous good fortune. Not to discount the remarkable ability of people to meet challenges, in the distant future some advances in equipment or technique which cannot even be imagined today might make runs at Niagara commonplace. But for now they are impossible. Although he had run a 60-foot drop on a small-volume stream, Jesse was not ready for this next step. Niagara Falls is three times as high and has 500 times the volume.

The media gave a lot of coverage to Jesse's foolishness. His crazy stunt made all the big city papers and was featured on the evening news. Since the performance of our world class slalom athletes and expert river runners is seldom covered by the media, while this sort of lunacy draws headlines, the public already thinks boaters are all little more than crazy thrill seekers, not participants in a physically and mentally challenging sport. Stunts like this reinforce all the worst stereotypes and make it harder for paddlers to gain access to more sensible sections of river, like Great Falls on the Potomac.

Boaters who would never consider running Niagara Falls or any other crazy run that calls for forgetting their river sense and performing one quick act of bravado may exhibit instead an attitude on rivers that can be summed up in the saying, "It's only water. Everything's bound to work out." And, of course, it usually does. After all, rivers are usually forgiving of error, as long as it is not too flagrant. But when the same error is repeated for long enough, eventually the bill comes due. Consider, for example, a very skilled boater who has a habit of saying, "I can take care of myself. Just go after my gear." Bob Taylor, who died one late summer day in 1977 in Lost Paddle Rapid on the Gauley River, was such a boater.

Bob Taylor

Bob Taylor, 34, was considered by his peers to be the finest boater of his day in West Virginia and one of the best in the East. Being an amateur runner of no small achievement as well as someone who took his boating seriously enough to train for it, he was in top physical condition. He had a reliable roll, good technical skills, and a fine feel for the water. He was experienced on both small and big rivers and during the past ten years had made many noteworthy descents. But the Gauley was his favorite river; he ran it often and at all levels and knew each drop intimately. Those who boated with him praised his judgment and looked to him for leadership. Others who had not boated with him, but knew him by reputation only, occasionally questioned the propriety of some of his exploits, but these judgments, often born of envy, are common among paddlers.

Lost Paddle Rapid, where the accident took place, lies just downstream from the mouth of the Meadow River. It is a long, tricky class IV-V rapid requiring numerous tight turns in powerful, pushy water.

Most ominous are the many undercut rocks, where numerous paddles have disappeared. "Paddle this one at low water," some say, "and you'll never want to paddle it again." In the 70's, boaters often speculated when it would claim its first body.

Bob's party on the day of the accident consisted of five people, all solid paddlers, and included several who knew the river almost as well as he did. Bob was in fine form, paddling the river aggressively, joking with his friends, and surfing waves and holes at every opportunity. Above Lost Paddle, the Meadow's flow brought the level to 3100 cfs. Entering the rapid, the boaters ran the first two drops without incident. At the bottom of the second drop, part of the party continued ahead while others remained to watch Bob surf the smaller of the holes. Bob was well known for his surfing ability, so no one thought it unusual when he moved on to the second and larger hole. Here he got a very rough ride; he flipped and rolled, flipped and rolled, while still maintaining fair control. Following the third flip, he may have decided that the smartest thing to do was swim out; he may have lost his breath. No one knows. He recirculated once in the hole and then flushed out.

Bob was a strong swimmer and did not mind swimming rapids. Even so, Leo Bode, a good paddler who knew the river well, immediately went to Bob's rescue. He extended his stern grab loop and pulled Bob toward an eddy on river left. About four feet from the eddyline, Bob let go and swam for safety. As he did, he forced Leo to take an obstructed path to avoid hitting him. For a moment, Leo lost sight of Bob. At the bottom of the rapid, members of the party collected Bob's boat and paddle and waited for him to walk down the shore. When he did not appear, they began searching the riverbank, a task made slow by the rugged terrain and the dense undergrowth. About half an hour later, someone spotted a faint orange blur beneath the surface of the water.

Although his body was quite close to the bank, it was impossible to get to because of the speed and power of the water. With the realization that Bob was beyond its help, the group sent for aid. State Police divers and volunteers got a rope attached to his body that afternoon but had to stop as darkness approached. That night the water level dropped to around 2100 cfs. In the morning, the officers were able to remove a small log, allowing Bob's body to float free and be recovered. Bob's foot might have been caught, but no one knows for sure. This is a likely guess; the drop upstream was steep, which would have made it difficult for Bob to keep his feet high in the obstructed, technical whitewater. At such times, tucking into a ball gives a swimmer a better chance of flushing through.

The most serious and the perhaps fatal error in Bob's case was that he let go of his rescuer when he needed help most—not in the unobstructed center of the river but in the left side of the fourth drop of Lost Paddle Rapid, where the river is lined with huge, undercut boulders. There are times when a victim should let go of a rescuer, but this was not one of those times. For rescuers, it is important to remember that a swimmer is not safe until he or she reaches shore; if you dump a swimmer into an eddy, sheer exhaustion may allow him or her to be pulled back out into the main current. Along the same lines, swimmers should generally cooperate with rescues even if they don't really need them; after all, how else are others going to get the rescue practice they need? Bear in mind, of course, that rescues can be dangerous, as anyone with much experience can attest. Here, as in other aspects of boating, paddlers have to weigh the risks.

Let us not, however, overlook other factors that contributed to this accident. A boater does not have to make one big mistake or commit one big error of judgment to die on a river; a number of minor errors can gang up with the same effect. Since few of us can boast that we have not made the same errors that Bob made and paid for so dearly, it will pay us to analyze our habits in light of the accident. Often, expert paddlers are not watched as closely as inexperienced ones, resulting in fewer precautions or delayed rescue attempts. Although not normal on trips with experienced boaters, additional precautions may help in a circumstance where self-rescue by swimming is difficult or especially dangerous. Many experts make lousy victims. While there is no substitute for self-rescue by rolling or strong swimming, in many cases accepting assistance spells the difference between routine and tragedy. Also, it must be noted that playing in a hole in the middle of a major rapid adds risk. Even an expert paddler has physical limits. Failure to pace oneself may lead to physical and mental exhaustion, bringing slower reflexes and poor judgment. Through varying circumstances, an expert paddler playing in a familiar river may end up in unexplored channels that hold great danger, and the paddler will be without the help of the cold calculation that marks the first run of the main chutes.

This accident affected the thinking of all paddlers who heard of it. There was a realization that a life vest, helmet, training, and the presence of other boaters do not give us a license to do whatever we want on a river. All rivers, difficult ones such as the Gauley as well as easier ones, contain dangerous traps, and we must act accordingly. We must emphasize teamwork, become ever more adept at rescue, and be constantly alert to the possibility that someone, including ourselves, may be making the first in a dangerous series of errors. It is a good policy always to leave a margin for miscalculations as you paddle, whenever you can, although this advice will forever be ignored by some. And when someone tells you to leave and go chase gear, remember to save people first!

The preceding account tells of the strongest member of a paddling group who perhaps goes too far, plays too hard, takes swims a bit too casually, and dies. But the weakest member of a party also faces special dangers. Weak members of a trip who go ahead with a run for which they are barely competent, because of either a general lack of skill or a temporary (and sometimes inexplicable) spell of mishaps or near misses, should consider not only the danger to themselves, but also the added danger, and of course trouble, that their companions will have to accept. Sitting out a run is hard, but anyone who has ever walked a rapid understands the reasons to do it. It is best to think carefully ahead of time, since sometimes boaters, like the one below, are given no chance to reevaluate their choices.

Charlie Walbridge, a member of this boating party, describes the accident, and he tells of the aftermath for the survivors.

Chuck Rawlins

"On July 11, 1982, I was with a group of eastern paddlers who decided to attempt the Golden Canyon of the South Fork of the Clearwater, near Golden, Idaho. The Upper South Fork is considered one of the toughest runs in the entire state: steep, rocky, and relentless for miles. Also, significantly, it is very deceptive when viewed from the road that runs alongside. One of the members of our group, 45-year-old Chuck Rawlins, was an experienced boater with runs throughout the East and a Grand Canyon trip the previous year. However, he was not in exceptional physical condition. During the past season, he had been having trouble with his roll, and on this western trip, which ended on the Clearwater, he had swum on every river.

"We arrived at the Clearwater after a week on the rivers in the Payette drainage. On the shuttle up, we remarked that the run looked eastern in character, estimating the water flow at 700 cfs. We identified several steep sections that would demand scouting and memorized important landmarks for future recognition. Playing it safe, we put in about two miles above the steep section so that we would have some warm-up prior to the descent.

"Well above the first drop, our group, including Chuck, pulled out to scout, with all members on shore except two, who continued downstream to catch a lower eddy to save time walking or carrying. I was scouting the lower portion of the drop when the shout came that Chuck was out of his boat. Chuck, having reentered the river without scouting, blew by the group in the lower eddy. I was carrying a throw bag and rushed to assist. I made a good throw. Chuck grabbed the bag itself, and the rope paid out to its full length as he was washed downstream. When the rope ran out, Chuck began to pendulum in to shore, but he swung into a hole. The hole was not dangerous in itself, but the force of the current in the eddy behind it held Chuck underwater and kept him from reaching shore. Finally, Chuck passed out, letting go of the rope; he washed into a tree at the bottom of a small eddy on the far side of the river.

"Our group mobilized itself to help Chuck but had trouble because of the rugged country. I tried to flag down cars to take me back to my boat but was thwarted by apathy or lack of comprehension on the part of the drivers. Eventually a fisherman drove me to the top of the drop. I threw my boat into the back of his truck and then drove downstream to a point opposite Chuck. The rapids were still hard class IV, and I was blown downstream about fifty yards on my ferry attempt. In the meantime, another paddler walked down the far shore from the head of the drop. He reached Chuck first and easily pulled him free from the log. When I arrived, we started CPR. We continued for more than an hour.

"Two other members of the group began working to get a line across the river. The police and ambulance, eventually summoned by passersby, arrived. Rescue personnel were assisted by two rock climbers in setting up a Tyrolean traverse. One climber went over to help attach lines to the victim, and rescuers pulled Chuck across the river. The paddlers carried their boats to safe places and ferried across to the roadside. Chuck was rushed to the Grangeville Hospital, where he was pronounced dead."

Charlie Walbridge went on to say, "People need to be prepared for the aftereffects of such a distresssing event. I still think about Chuck's death often. I can still see his face when I threw him the rope, and how his body floated passively when he let go minutes later. I remember how Al and I prompted each other to help remember the steps of CPR; how heavy his body felt; how terrified I was. And I know what I would do differently if confronted with the same situation today.

"I also remember how hard it was to talk about what happened. The sheriff, whom we went to afterwards, shrugged his shoulders and said, 'That's the second one this year, boys.' Apparently a fisherman had fallen into the river a few weeks earlier. I talked for a long time with one fellow before he left for home the next day. That night, instead of sleeping next to the river, I bedded down near the highway, where I could hear the traffic noise.

"The next day the group's strongest boater broached on a rock in a class III, flipped, swam, and came up with two broken fingers. One boater left for Las Vegas, sold all his gear, and has never been seen on a river again. A couple traveling together broke up soon afterwards. Another member of the group called me five years later, after another accident, not to talk about the most recent event but the one we had been involved with five years earlier.

"After taking two days off I tried to boat again but was too tense to have any fun. Easy rapids made me jumpy. I almost lost my boat when I dropped it on a steep slope from the take-out; a member of another party had to chase it for over two miles. It was time to go home.

"I went to the funeral a week later. My friends and I cried even though several of us were angry at Chuck for being such a dummy. We looked down at the open coffin and joked that Chuck had never been so well groomed in real life. I paddled some easy whitewater later that summer, but nothing hard. I couldn't believe that a careful, conservative person like myself had been involved with something like this, or that with all my training I couldn't have saved him. I vowed to be less intense on the water myself.

"That fall, for the first time since 1971 and the only season to date, I didn't paddle the Gauley. I was packing when I got a call that someone had drowned in Initiation. It made me feel sick to my stomach, and I knew I wasn't ready. Later that winter during a rare December warm spell I ran the Tygart, one of my favorite rivers. Although it was an uneventful trip, I was totally exhausted afterwards. But it broke the spell; the next spring I was able to get back into paddling hard again.

"A fatal accident is always terribly upsetting to those involved, and doubly so if the victim is personally known to you. You need to be prepared for some unpleasant aftereffects, which will vary from person to person. I got psychological help over that summer, and I'd recommend that to anyone. Outfitters tell me that a state or county mental health worker may be available to your group. The Critical Incident Stress Foundation, (5018 Dorsey Hall Drive #104, Ellicott City, MD 21042; hotline number 410/313-2473) is a nationwide group set up to offer insight and support to those who have participated in a failed rescue. A three-hour debriefing, done by trained volunteers at no cost to you, is almost totally effective in preventing critical incident stress. That's the term for the turmoil I felt following Chuck's death.

"Still, I will never paddle a river with the same complete assurance again.

"I don't know why Chuck ran this drop without looking at it first, but he had a tendency to follow others, assuming he would make it either in his boat or out. Paddlers should make their own decisions, of course, and one of the decisions a paddler must be prepared to make is when to carry. While the advice of friends is helpful, boaters on expert trips must know their limits and act accordingly, must be able to scout a drop and decide whether to run it. Many paddlers felt that someone should have advised Chuck, who had lost a boat on the Middle Fork of the Salmon and was outfitting a new one during this shuttle, not to make this run. None in our group expected him to, given the trouble he had been having. But he declined when asked to shuttle the last vehicle downstream.

"Concerning the specifics of the accident and rescue attempts, since Chuck was only ten to fifteen feet from shore, grabbing the rope, not the bag, would have probably kept him out of the hole, a lesson that most experienced paddlers know today. Or I could have simply thrown him less rope. The rope's swinging him into a hole created an unusual situation, but a second rescuer could have worked his way down the rescue line, hand over hand, pulling Chuck ashore. Chuck also could have aided in his rescue by rolling onto his back and holding the rope over one shoulder. This would have allowed him to float faceup. CPR was prompt and well done, but the terrain and weight of the victim created difficulties. Police and rescue squad personnel were not trained in advanced rescue techniques, but in remote areas, this is not unusual. It is unrealistic to depend on aid from passersby."

As much as possible a party should be self-contained, able to make energetic and concerted group rescue efforts. Rescue skills should be practiced, and boaters need to recertify CPR frequently for optimum effect. Help, when available, in the form of other groups, passersby, or well-trained rescue personnel, is a godsend but cannot be counted on. This is part of the risk of whitewater, a risk that increases with increasingly difficult and remote runs.

Although all boaters face risk, the most vulnerable person is the hanger-on—the weakest member of the party or a usually strong paddler not in top form that day—or someone who exhibits a pattern of behavior that subjects him or her to unnecessary dangers. In the past, although dire consequences were often predicted, a swim on an expert-level run, while unpleasant, was seldom fatal. In today's difficult whitewater, this is no longer true. In the past decade, paddlers have greatly extended the limits of the possible in our sport, some say by as much as two classes. The result has been a tendency to devaluate the difficulty of the old standards, leading to dangerous confusion between, for example, old class V's and new class V's, a confusion especially dangerous to paddlers willing to make runs above their skill level in the belief that all will work out right.

In addition to having an off day, which all boaters have, or even an off season for which no cause is clear, physical impairments commonly compromise skill and clear judgment. It is a rare boater who will admit to being too cold, hungry, or tired to function at top levels, yet these factors define many trips where there is only a limited amount of time to do as much boating as possible. Sickness and injury, of course, also affect one's ability to make good decisions. And bullheadedness also plays its part—once we've driven 300 miles, we're darn sure going to boat something. Sometimes, for these reasons, good, clear-headed paddlers make poor decisions and execute them poorly. If all had turned out well in the end during the following run, Charlie Deaton would have had a funny story to tell for years to come. Unfortunately, he did not have that opportunity.

Charlie Deaton

On the last Saturday in March 1989, four experienced paddlers began a late afternoon run on the Lower Blackwater River below North Fork Junction after an unsuccessful attempt on a steep tributary leading to the same spot. The Lower Blackwater is one of West Virginia's classic expert runs, starting off as a series of class IV-V rapids, with the most difficult drops occurring at the beginning. The victim, Charlie Deaton, 59, was a solid paddler with wide experience in West Virginia. The other paddlers, Whitney Shields, Jim Snyder, and Eric Lindberg, were also extremely strong and had run the river the previous day when it was a few inches lower.

The group had begun the day at 10:30 A.M. with an attempt on the North Fork, a small tributary of the Blackwater that parallels the railroad tracks leading to the Blackwater put-in. Once committed to the effort, they found the creek to be an endless series of unrunnable waterfalls. After many hours of portaging, they retreated hundreds of feet back up the steep bank to the railroad tracks. Working steadily, they arrived at the Blackwater put-in at 3:30. There they had lunch, but Charlie chose not to eat; he had recovered from colon surgery and was afraid the food would upset his stomach. Deciding to run the Lower Blackwater, they faced a late start, not unreasonable if the group adopted a no-nonsense approach that included quickly portaging, rather than scouting, the major drops. The following description of the run and the accident that followed was submitted by Jim Snyder and is edited only slightly for clarity's sake.

"We quickly portaged the first of five big rapids. The next drop, a five-foot ledge, was visible from there. We had to run down a short way and catch a left eddy to portage. I got there first and found a sneak route. I was coming around the drop when I saw Charlie coming over the falls. At the base he flipped really hard and was able to pull away from the hole a bit before he bailed out. I was right there when he surfaced; he grabbed my boat and I paddled him to shore. He held onto his own boat and paddle, minimizing rescue efforts. He sat for five minutes on shore before continuing; he said he was tired, but he wasn't breathing hard and was quick to get back in his boat.

"In a short while we reached the third big rapid, Rock and Roll.

We eddied out on the left, then ferried to the right side of the river to scout. Charlie lost his ferry angle and was swept into the rapid. He paddled extremely well to the bottom, where he pinned between two large rocks. He got out of his boat, pulled his equipment free, grinned, and shrugged his shoulders. I told him that he needed to be more careful about catching eddies, but he told me that he knew that and that I should lighten up and not worry about him.

"I described the next rapid to him, a class III approach above a couple of class IV holes. There were four eddies to catch, and I pointed them out. In his run he made the first three, but he fell over trying to cross the river to the fourth, right above the first large hole. I was with him and tried to bump his boat into shore as he set up to roll. He rolled most of the way up, but his paddle was on the upstream side and the current pushed him under. I couldn't follow him, so I watched as he ran through the first two holes and exited his boat. I paddled down next to him and told him to swim to the right to avoid being swept into Slide Rapid just downstream. He swam very hard into water six to twelve inches deep but was too tired to get his footing. He slipped and washed down the slide.

"I knew that the slide was shallow (less than five inches deep through most of its hundred-yard length) and assumed he would eventually stop in the shallow water. Eric arrived, nearly hitting Charlie's boat as he ran the hole next to it. The boat popped free as he passed, and he pushed it, full of water, towards me on the right. I knew I wouldn't be able to complete the rescue in my boat, so I jumped out and chased Charlie's kayak down the slide and picked it up near the bottom. Eric was committed to the slide after pushing the boat over, and I yelled to Eric to look for Charlie. He thought Charlie was on shore upstream of the slide where I had landed, and he could not really hear over the roar of the rapids.

"Just then I saw Charlie wash or swim onto a rock several hundred yards downstream of the slide. He was seemingly sitting calmly, but his head was rolling from side to side. I yelled to Eric to give chase, but he still didn't know Charlie was in trouble and thought I was pointing out Charlie's paddle. It was very hard to see because the river runs due west into the glare of the setting sun. After about twenty seconds Charlie slipped off the rock and disappeared. Whitney and I ran the slide, meeting Eric heading upstream with his spare paddle for Charlie to use. It was only then that he found out that Charlie was in trouble downstream.

"I gave chase and ten minutes later found Charlie's body. It was caught between two shallow rocks, belly-down underwater. Charlie had a bad bruise over his right eye from an impact with a rock. I quickly jumped out of my boat, recovered the body, and began CPR. In the next five to ten minutes, Whitney and Eric showed up to help. We worked on Charlie for twenty to twenty-five minutes before it was clear that the concussion was fatal. There was no sign of water in his lungs.

"It was then approximately 5:15 P.M., some forty-five minutes after the accident. It would be dark in a little over an hour, and we had eight miles of whitewater to run. We brought Charlie's body to the right shore. Whitney climbed to the railroad tracks, marked the spot, and headed downstream on foot. Eric and I finished the run at 6:00 P.M. and notified authorities. The body was evacuated by 11:00 P.M. It took over an hour to bring it to the tracks 300 feet above the river."

Jim believes that the victim hit his head in one of the two holes above the slide and that the blow was probably fatal. The impact centered on the right cheekbone and temple; massive swelling and bleeding from the right eye indicated a very serious and possibly fatal concussion. Doctors say that someone with a concussion often seems okay initially but loses strength and consciousness as internal bleeding puts pressure on the brain. A heavier helmet than Charlie's lightweight Ace, intended for racing and easy paddling, might have reduced the injury.

At the time, Charlie's decision to attempt the run seemed natural, but in light of the accident, the victim's choice appears questionable. His age, combined with health problems that limited his food and water intake, and the strenuous day of portaging on the North Fork made the sustained effort required on the Blackwater difficult, and his resultant lack of boat control contributed directly to his injury. Although backing out of a run, especially one in a deep gorge with poor access, is always difficult, it is an option that Charlie should have taken when it became clear that he could no longer control his kayak.

During the accident, the difficulty of the river greatly hindered communication between the rescuers, and the group lost sight of the victim for a short time. Had he not hit his head, these few seconds probably would have made no difference, but in this case they might have, although his head injury was so severe that even immediate help could have been in vain. It is, however, a lesson that a group this strong can misplace someone for a few minutes. Even when a boater is paddling with an experienced party, there are times when he or she is out of reach of help, and at these times the consequences of errors in judgment or control are compounded.

Since a key rule of rescue is to assist people before recovering equipment, the boat rescue at the head of the slide is open to question. The steps taken by the group were probably reasonable on this steep, technical river in that they did not slow pursuit by more than a few seconds. Eric pursued with all possible speed by running the slide without scouting, and Jim ran down the slide on foot. To keep an eye on a swimmer every second in difficult water is not always possible and is one of the risks of attempting such runs.

Once Charlie was found, CPR was begun quickly. In a wilderness setting, the prognosis for someone who does not respond quickly to this treatment is not good, since advanced life support becomes necessary because of chemical changes in the victim's body. To have stayed longer with nightfall approaching held risks for the survivors, who barely got out before dark.

Unfortunately, as is often the case, avoiding the problem entirely was the only option that would have assured success. The primary cause of the accident was Charlie Deaton's willingness to continue the run despite his physical problems, inability to eat, and skill-reducing fatigue. Runs of this difficulty require uncompromised skill; to attempt them in impaired physical condition is to accept grave personal risk. In hindsight, the accident could have been prevented if the group had recognized Charlie's debilitating exhaustion and its effects on his judgment and insisted that he leave the trip. However, this is a difficult and unusual step on a trip undertaken by adults of equal ability, and paddlers must not be in the habit of relying on others to make decisions for them. In theory, it is possible to refuse to allow someone you suspect to be suffering impaired judgment to continue on a river trip. In practice, this is nearly impossible to do with friends.

We depend on our paddling partners to make the proper choices for themselves, but this does not always happen. Charlie Deaton misjudged his condition and his ability to perform at the level required by the run. Although not directly attributable to physical problems, Chuck Rawlins, in the previous account, and Jack, who committed to a wilderness kayak trip for which he was unprepared (Chapter 2), also misjudged their abilities, an error all boaters have probably made but for which these three paid a high penalty.

Some decisions turn out to be just plain wrong, and no physical impairment can be used to explain them. In the following brief account, both the victim, a guide in the Grand Canyon, and his party show a notable lack of concern for a situation that proves fatal. Given their experience, we must wonder at the victim's casual approach to danger and at his companions' evident nonchalance.

Martin Hunsucker

Martin Hunsucker, 54, a guide with Georgie's Royal River Rats, drowned in June 1989, following a capsizing in Crystal Rapid, one of the biggest drops in Arizona's Grand Canyon. The victim was running a thirty-three-foot S-Rig with a commercial party, which scouted the drop and entered the rapid on river left. Here the engine died; the craft was forced up against a rock wall on river left, where it capsized. All crew members, with the exception of Martin, climbed back on the boat and began pulling passengers aboard. Martin gave his fellow guides a thumbs-up sign, indicating that he was okay, and then he apparently swam downstream in search of a passenger. The remaining guides assumed he would be all right, and even when a head count showed Martin was missing, they guessed that he had been picked up by another boat cruising in the area. Without knowing for sure where he was, the rest of the guides repaired the boat and headed downstream. Martin's body was spotted by another outfitter shortly thereafter, and a doctor on that trip pronounced him dead. His party, which was camped downstream, was notified of the fatality that evening.

The area downstream of Crystal Rapid is fast and turbulent for miles, with a flow of about 12,000 cfs the day of the accident. In addition, the water was 54 degrees, quite a shock to a person who moments earlier had been basking in the 110-degree desert air. Grand Canyon guides wear no wet suits; the heat of the air, combined with the fact that their rigs seldom flip, makes wearing protective clothing impractical. Therefore, swimmers are vulnerable to hypothermia following the rare capsizings, and efforts must focus on getting them out of the water promptly. Evidently the cold, turbulent river proved to be too much for Martin. In retrospect, it was a poor idea on his part to swim after a passenger under these conditions. As it turned out, his efforts were unnecessary; all clients were picked up downstream.

The fact that Martin's disappearance was not cause for alarm to his party until evening raises disturbing questions as to the mechanisms used by his group to keep track of people after a flip. It is hard to imagine a professional guide leaving his own trip on another group's boat without first informing his party, although this is exactly what his fellow guides surmised. A more likely scenario is that Martin could have been marooned against a cliff somewhere downstream and been in need of help. It would have been better for his group to initiate a thorough search of the area when he turned up missing. There must have been a point when Martin realized that his choice to swim had been a bad one. During this brief, lonely time, he probably wished fervently for assistance. At a crucial time, help, even of a minor nature, may spell the difference between rescue and tragedy, as is amply made clear in the following chilling account.

Donna Berglund

Dr. Donna Berglund, former member of the U.S. Whitewater Team and a much-loved paddling companion of many, died late one evening in June 1986, on the Swan River in Montana. The Swan, generally considered class IV, is small and continuous, similar to the Savage River but narrower and with fewer eddies. Donna was in the area training for a race. After making a late afternoon run, she wanted to take another. Unable to find anyone to go with her, she characteristically decided to go alone.

She probably spun out on a midstream boulder, but this is not certain. What is certain, however, is that she ended up pinned heads-up against a sunken log. Early the next morning, the first racers on the river found her in this position. The pin was not severe and was easily released. She probably died from hypothermia.

No single incident better illustrates the dangers of solo paddling. Donna, an expert river runner with years of experience in a wildwater boat, made a minor error in boat control. She could have been rescued easily by even one other person. It is likely that she had plenty of time as the dark settled in to think about her situation and to consider her decision to boat alone.

While the pleasures of solo boating are many and often subtle, so too are the risks. In some places regulations attempt to keep solo boaters off the rivers, an attempt that may be seen as an infringement on individual rights. But many boaters believe that the risks of boating solo outweigh the pleasures and that regulations designed to discourage the practice, which, it must be admitted, makes whitewater boating significantly more dangerous than it has to be, are a reasonable act by agencies charged with protecting the public. Skill and experience, important though they are, cannot totally counter the special risks of solo boating, as the above account illustrates.

The brevity of the record, due of course to the fact that there were no witnesses, stands in sharp contrast to the long hours Donna Berglund must have had to relive every detail. One wonders if the victim in the account below, who died in Washington State, had even as much of an understanding of his fate as the following sketchy reconstruction provides us.

Bezuk

The victim, reported only as Bezuk, was a 52-year-old Hungarian refugee who escaped his native country driving a captured Russian tank. In addition to being a boater, he was a sky diver, rock climber, and pilot. He worked as a bridge tender in the Seattle area, and, because of his work schedule, seldom had weekends off. Therefore, he usually boated alone. He had paddled rivers around the world, including the Amazon River, on which he made a 3500-mile descent in 1970 and was a strong, accomplished boater who had run the Green River many times. Local paddlers felt he was as mentally and physically tough as any boater in the area and said he was the only one to run class V rivers solo on a regular basis. They also said he was a difficult man, with a strong personality, and few went out of their way to paddle with him. No one knows what happened on the day he died.

The Green River Gorge is a popular run for Seattle-area paddlers. At 7500 cfs, the area around the Nozzle is very fast and powerful, approaching class V difficulty because of the lack of rescue spots.

Each of us
has the freedom
to decide which
risks we accept and
which we avoid...

There is a river-wide, sneakable hole at the Nozzle, and this is probably where Bezuk met his demise. Park officials at Palmer-Kanasket State Park initiated a search with local boaters after noticing that his car had been in the parking lot too long. Kayakers discovered him in an eddy between the Nozzle and the take-out at Franklin Bridge. Rangers reported a massive injury to the head around the left eye. This injury, following a flip, may have precipitated his death.

Of the well-documented risks of solo boating, not the least is that there is no one to help you if you get in trouble. Sometimes, however, there is nothing other boaters could do. No one will ever know if another paddler might have made a difference to Bezuk, but it is clear that he understood the risks of paddling alone and was fully willing to deal with them. While this behavior cannot be recommended, neither, in some circles, is whitewater paddling. Each of us has the freedom to decide which risks we will accept and which we will avoid. Bezuk clearly was a man who valued this freedom and chose to accept the risks that came with challenging himself.

4

Like the preceding ones, accidents highlight the risks involved in solo boating, where in case of problems there is no one to give aid of any sort. Realizing this, most paddlers boat with at least one partner, coming to know each other's skills and nature. Two-person trips are common, and the bond that grows between two boaters is strong. However, boating in pairs may put the sole rescuer in a position where options are limited by factors going well beyond lack of strength or virtual inability to use even basic rope systems, such as a snag line, where at least two rescuers are required. The solo rescuer often must face difficult decisions, since only one rescue technique may be tried at a time. Multiple efforts, which it is hoped complement one another, may be tried only if more people are on the rescue scene. Of course, it is possible that too many people at an accident site may lead to simple confusion, to uncoordinated efforts due to a diffusion of leadership, or, in rare cases, to dissension and strife among rescuers with different ideas. But rescues with more personnel are more often successful and also safer for those involved than solo attempts, where limited options may lead to the solo rescuer's taking desperate chances to save his or her paddling partner.

Often the relationship between the two boaters who paddle together is very close, and during an accident the most agonizing decision is whether it is better to attempt a rescue alone, even though the chances for success are very slim, or to leave one's companion to go for help, even though the chances are great that help will come too late. In the following three accounts, separate accidents involving pairs of boaters, this central dilemma is faced by rescuers; the fate of the three victims hangs in the balance. The close relationship between boaters gives these accounts a wealth of painful detail and a completeness of narrative shot through with the sorrow of what cannot be done.

Chris

The weekend of March 15 saw the East's first warm day of the 1986 season and very high water. Runs in southern Virginia were up, and Chris and Eric put in on the North River, a small tributary of the Shenandoah, which can be paddled only when the water is high.

This was an early-season run, and despite the unseasonably warm day, the water temperature was estimated at 40 degrees. The North River was in a normal seasonal flood with water in the trees on both banks. Although for the most part a two-boat trip, the two had been joined by an open boater who took off earlier than they did. Both of the continuing paddlers were in decked boats, which were more maneuverable on the small stream. Even though the river was very high, neither felt a sense of any great danger in continuing their run.

Chris had been paddling open boats all his life and had been kayaking for a year and a half, virtually every weekend. He was still getting used to a new Prijon T-Slalom, but earlier in the day he had had no trouble making the moves demanded by the North. Eric had paddled both OC-1 and C-1 extensively on eastern rivers during the past several years. In addition, Eric had been very involved in Canoe Cruisers Association safety activities and had led a weekly practice group the summer before.

Both paddlers wore life jackets and helmets and were reasonably well prepared for cold water. Chris wore a dry suit with a heavy pile sweatshirt and long pants. Eric wore a Farmer John wet suit with the knees cut out and two light polypro shirts and light polypro pants. In his boat Eric carried a throw rope and a light pruning saw. Neither had experience on the North. Eric had extensive experience on small streams; Chris did not.

The accident happened about 5:00 P.M. in the vicinity of a sweeping left-hand bend near a local landmark, Chimney Rocks, which juts out river right and may have placed some of the obstacles in shadow. As the two rounded the bend, they saw that the stream broke into two channels around a flooded, tree-covered island. The right channel was obstructed by a fallen tree; the left seemed clear. There were no rapids in the area, just very swift, strong current.

The paddlers drifted around the bend, making the necessary move to river left, neither working especially hard at it. Then, without warning, Chris ran into the trees and was pinned upright in midstream. At once Eric began maneuvering to maintain his position and to move to the site of the problem. He ferried to river right, talking with Chris, who was struggling, possibly in an effort to get out of his boat. But the current swept Eric downstream into the right channel where the strainer waited. Erik reached high and grabbed some limbs, exiting his boat and climbing into the tree. He tried to hang onto his boat, but it broached upstream, filled with water, and was washed away.

Eric heard Chris say something, and turning, Eric saw that Chris had been rolled to his downstream side and was trapped in his boat. No water was breaking over the midsection of his boat, and he had grabbed a tree behind him to hold himself above the water.

It was immediately apparent that the situation was serious, that Chris's life was in danger. The strong current bore directly on the boat, pinning it firmly. Chris was trapped in midstream, partly immersed in the cold river.

Eric, on the bank with no equipment, had essentially three choices. First, he could try to swim to the site of the pin in midstream. Second, he could try to locate his boat and retrieve his rope and saw. Third, he could go for help, leaving the victim. He opted to look for his boat, which he found downstream, but he judged that his chances of getting to it were poor. Returning to the accident site, he judged that his chances of reaching Chris were also poor. Additionally, he thought that dislodging the boat or otherwise effecting a rescue would probably be impossible without mechanical assistance, and he could locate no branches or limbs to use as levers.

Reluctantly, he left Chris and ran for ten minutes to a farmhouse where a call was placed to the Bridgewater Volunteer Rescue Squad. He could find no rope at the farm and, with three teenagers he hailed on the way, returned to the site, where the situation had clearly deteriorated.

Water was now breaking over the entire boat. Either the water was rising or the boat was slipping down the trees. Weakened by cold, Chris was having trouble keeping his head above water. Eric entered the water and on his second try succeeded in swimming to Chris. He was able to stand in the water and support the victim, who was semiconscious, but he was unable to dislodge the boat. Not willing to give up his attempts knowing that help was on its way, he divided his time between supporting Chris and trying to free the boat.

The first member of the rescue squad arrived on the scene about twenty minutes after the call. By this time, the exhausted Chris was losing consciousness. A rope was tied to the bow of the pinned boat, but efforts to pull it free were unsuccessful. Additional members of the squad arrived and used a rope to get a member experienced in scuba diving to the boat. Eric was directed to leave the water at this point.

Chris was limp in the water, his eyes dilated, and apparently was no longer breathing. Initial attempts to effect his rescue from the pin, although well executed, failed. Finally, Chris's body was removed from the boat at around 9:00 P.M. Attempts at resuscitation did not revive him.

The dangers inherent in two-boat parties underlie every aspect of this tragedy. If another paddler had been along, different choices would have been available in the early stages of the pin, and a different outcome might have resulted. Because of Eric's disposition and training, he happened to have equipment that might have allowed prompt rescue. Once Eric's boat was gone, however, there was no backup equipment or extra boat to salvage the stranded gear. Small parties are tempting and convenient, but they do multiply dangers and complicate rescues. Extra hands had to be sent for, and the victim could not be stabilized during this period.

Once they arrived on the scene, the Bridgewater team's response and techniques were sophisticated and appropriate. Even though the rescuers were not successful, several points need to be made. First, no one else died. In the conditions of that day, all rescuers were at serious risk. One misstep or misjudgment on Eric's part could have quickly turned this accident into a double tragedy. Second, the efforts that were made are a tribute to the courage and training of all involved. In the past, whitewater boaters have sometimes found themselves at odds with inexperienced, unskilled rescuers, but not this time. The options available in this case were limited, but they were fully developed by rescuers at the scene.

In the next account, from Tennessee, another two-boat run turns bad, and another paddler must attempt a rescue solo. Ron Stewart's gripping, first-person record of the rescue attempt follows, edited only slightly for clarity's sake.

Mike Culbertson

"Suck Creek in southeast Tennessee is a very difficult run with a high gradient, and it is extremely congested with boulder jumbles and steep drops. Rains the previous evening had brought the creek to a low/medium level. Debris in the creek from storms, major floods, and roadwork make the run highly technical and difficult at any water level.

"By 1987, Mike and I had been paddling together for four years. We had kayaked extensively throughout the U.S., and during the summer of '86, in Europe. Mike was a well-respected paddler, with eight years' experience. He and I had paddled many of the steep runoff creeks in the Chattanooga area, such as the North Chicka-mauga Creek Gorge. The air temperature was warm for February. The water was cold but not frigid, and we were wearing cold-water gear. We still had good daylight. I had past training in first aid and CPR and am a Red Cross instructor.

"A major paved road parallels Suck Creek at a short but steep distance from the streambed. I had run the creek at lower water two weeks earlier with another boater (several portages were required), and it had also been run by two other paddlers. We had scouted the run on previous occasions and had removed some of the trees blocking some routes. Since this was Mike's first descent, I was leading most of the way.

"We had completed the upper third of the run and were running well, though we were a bit pushed on some of the technical turns. Overall, we felt good. We were on our toes, a bit anxious, as was normal for runs of this nature. Most scouting was of the eddy-hop variety, though we had scouted two previous rapids out of our boats, setting up a rope on one.

"We were about to enter the most difficult part of the run. I remarked that our first portage was coming up after a small ledge. The ledge is actually a large, slightly submerged boulder on river right and an irregular chute to the left of center. The total drop is about four feet. I approached cautiously, remembering a rock somewhere in the chute from my previous run. We both got out to scout, quickly agreed on a route to the left of center, and didn't think much of it. It was the kind of rapid (probably II+-III) we routinely ran many times on a difficult creek. I ran first, to the right of the tongue, at a slight angle, leaning a bit on my right, and eddied out to wait for Mike. I thought Mike's approach was too far to the left but still in the main flush. In retrospect I remember thinking the far left side looked a bit funny but didn't give it much thought. As he went over the drop, Mike just disappeared. I remember being stunned at how quickly he was gone. I paddled to the left bank, ran to the spot where he was, but still couldn't see him or his boat. Normally, in a pin situation, a plume of water will rooster-tail over the person, often forming an air pocket around the head. I saw no plume and believed no air pocket formed.

"My first impulse was to get to Mike in the water. I attempted to reach him from a large rock on the left, but the force of the water pushed me a short distance downstream into a left-side eddy near my boat. I retrieved my rope and ran back to where Mike was. I briefly saw his hands out of the water, but just before I threw my rope, the hands disappeared. The thrown rope was never taken. I attempted to reach him several times during the next few minutes, but each time I tried, I was flushed out. Being pushed into the eddy made repeated attempts possible without much time lost. I knew Mike had probably lost consciousness. I remember trying to figure out a way to effect a rescue so that CPR could be initiated in hopes of a cold-water reflex. Since no part of him or his boat was visible in the rushing water, this was difficult. I briefly considered some form of a tag line, but Mike's boat was so deep, and the force of the water was so strong, it would have been difficult to engage the rope under stern or bow. Being alone also limited the time and options with which I had to work. I continued trying to reach him in the water.

"After fifteen to twenty minutes I left the scene, paddled across the creek, ran up the hill, and tried unsuccessfully to wave down some passing motorists. I ran to some nearby trailer homes and was taken to one that had a telephone. I called 911. I know I was out of breath when I talked to the dispatcher. When I hung up, I asked the man with me if he would wait on the road till the rescue squad arrived and try to attract other help. I ran back to the site (it wasn't far from the road), paddled across, and continued my efforts. I tried to grab Mike's life jacket but couldn't reach it.

"I finally managed to grab his paddling jacket. I threaded my rope through it, making a loop. I pulled from the side, but the boat remained lodged. I threaded more rope and managed to get an angle where I could pull more to the upstream. After several attempts, the boat suddenly popped out, rolled up on its side, turned over, and floated free. Mike partially fell out. I jumped in, pulled him to shore, removed both his and my helmets, and began CPR.

"Ten to fifteen minutes after I started CPR, rescuers began to arrive. They had trouble crossing the creek, but some eventually reached us. They wanted to know how long Mike had been under-water. I told them about thirty minutes, and they said it was too late to revive him. Between breaths, I said it was possible a cold-water reflex had occurred and that we should keep trying. A sheriff's deputy arrived and radioed that CPR was in progress. I'm not sure exactly when the rescue squad arrived. By this time it was beginning to get dark. We continued CPR another thirty to forty-five minutes, at which point sheriff's department personnel brought a Stokes litter and Mike was transported to the opposite bank. Once on the other side, he was carried to an ambulance and taken to a county hospital. I thought the rescue team and people at the scene were all concerned and helpful, but I don't think they had much experience with swift-water rescue or cold-water drowning.

"Mike and I both knew the risks of kayaking difficult water, and though I believe it was a tragic accident involving a desperate, improbable situation, it has been hard to deal with the guilt of being unable to rescue my friend. As I've reconstructed the incident, many of those feelings have passed, and I believe there are lessons that can be taught that may help other paddlers in similar situations.

"Mike and I often paddled rivers together. Much of the pleasure we derived from paddling came from paddling by ourselves. We knew each other's abilities and style and worked well together as a team. In retrospect, if others had been present, I believe it would have increased the number of rescue options available. The force of the current at the entrapment was extremely strong, and it's speculative at best to consider a swimmer's being belayed at the point of a pin. One highly skilled paddler who visited the scene at low water said he felt if other people had been there, it probably wouldn't have made a difference. But since one person did eventually get the victim out, then with more people present, it's possible the rescue could have been effected faster and with more efficiency.

"Next, since I had to leave the scene to get help and managed to free Mike when I returned, had others been present, rescue attempts would not have been interrupted. While one or two went for help, the others could have continued their efforts, possibly freeing the victim and initiating CPR sooner.

"Another factor is the psychological impact of having more than one person at the scene during the rescue attempt. Reconstructing the scene and my actions, I don't recall panic, but I can't help but believe I experienced some form of shock and, ultimately, exhaustion, which may have affected my actions. Other people being present, as long as they had remained rational, would certainly have had a positive influence.

"Past experience in rescue situations leads me to believe that getting to a trapped person, rather than throwing a rope, is usually more effective, but each situation has to be assessed in light of the circumstances of the incident. My first impulse was to get to Mike, not to reach for my rope. But since his hands did surface at one point, had I initially thrown my rope instead of tried to reach him in the water, he might have been able to take the rope. Having to retrieve my rope and unsnap a prusik and carabiner cost valuable seconds. Another person present would have allowed for both options.

"I carried a prusik. It might have been possible to get the prusik to Mike so that he could loop it under his shoulder or merely hold on while I pulled. Again, this is speculative and the technique would have had to have been enacted almost immediately. Something like this had worked in a rescue of a pinned boater on Daddy's Creek, Tennessee, but in that situation the person had been stable with his head above water. Other paddlers were present, and I was able to get above and behind the victim and pass a rope down to him.

"Would more careful scrutiny of the rapid have alerted us to danger? Probably. At water levels similar to what we had that day, one can see from river left (we scouted on the right) a small rise followed by a definite dip in the water in the extreme left side of the rapid. Mike's line went from left to center of the chute. Mine was more to the right of the tongue. In the context of the other rapids and our paddling experience, we didn't give much thought to the rapid other than to avoid an obvious boulder to the right of center.

"In the weeks that have passed since the accident, I've had time to think about what happened and why. Mike and I considered ourselves 'safe' boaters, albeit we knew we were running difficult water with inherent risks. Our experience, abilities, and rescue skills were good. Why did they fail us in this case? Why, when we were being so cautious, should it have happened at such a relatively insignificant-looking place? Why Mike, when his skills, style, and attitude on the river were exemplary?

"My wife once said, 'Sometimes you can do it right, and it still goes wrong. It's not a matter of skill alone. Chances are that at some time, some place, something will go wrong no matter how careful you are.' I don't think we can eliminate all the risk, but awareness that very good boaters like Mike can die will minimize the chances of these tragedies happening again."

Ron's account of Mike's death is a tribute to their paddling relationship. They were partners, friends; they trusted each other. Then a wall of water came between them.

Several years before, on a much larger river, two other friends and boating companions played out another *pas de deux*. This time, because of the nature of the accident, an extended and unusual entrapment in a shallow but powerful hydraulic, the two men were able to communicate at least until fatigue, and eventually water, silenced one of them. The story, told by the other, is a vivid record of a fateful event occurring in the fall of 1983 on the Father of Waters, the Mississippi River.

Charlie Schulman

The Mississippi is the largest river in the U.S., but it has never been known for its whitewater. However, in the area around Chain of Rocks, below the bridge of the same name on the Illinois-Missouri border near St. Louis, Missouri, an assortment of bridge piers, low dams, and islands creates a number of enjoyable waves and holes at the right levels, usually in late summer or fall. Most of the action takes place a good distance from shore, as the river is extremely wide.

On an unseasonably warm October 6, Charlie Schulman, the victim, and Herman Smith, his companion, took an afternoon outing to this popular play spot. Both were experienced kayakers with solid rolls. They had boated extensively in the Southeast and were extremely familiar with the Chain of Rocks area. This was a regular weekend outing for these two men.

The two entered the river about 3:30 P.M. from the Illinois side, checked the midchannel gauge tower, and ferried to one play spot after another. Smith noted that his companion seemed less aggressive than usual but thought nothing about it. After an hour and a half of playing, the pair began to head for shore, using a route that requires considerable skill but that had been used without incident for nearly fifteen years. It involves a long ferry behind the boil line of a sizable hydraulic. This bare summary, however, does not capture the essence of the accident. What follows are the slightly edited words of the survivor, Herm Smith.

"As was my habitual custom, I warned Charlie to stay slightly below the boil line as we ferried to river right. The time was about 5:00 P.M. I heard him yell for help behind me, turned to view him, lost my concentration, and found myself drawn into the hydraulic as he had been. I tried surfing, but it was apparent that I would lose my energy too fast trying to stay in the boat. I knew from the accounts of other boaters who had been trapped here that it was possible to stand. I wet exited and saw Charlie standing some ten yards left of me in a deeper and more violent part of the hole.

"I had been told that the right side of the hole was not as strong and offered a possible escape. But the water pushed left towards the more dangerous part. Using my boat as leverage, I worked slowly left so I could discuss with Charlie my plan for getting out. I urged him to hold on to my boat for stability and told him that I felt we could crab-crawl slowly out of the hole. He nodded and started to grab my boat but lost his footing and got sucked down and came up gasping for breath. I encouraged him to follow me, but he only nodded and looked ahead, concentrating on staying on his feet.

"I was concerned about his inaction. I discussed trying to dive down under the hydraulic to escape. I tried twice, but the attempts were sapping too much strength. We were slowly being drawn to the worst part of the hole. I urged him to move to the right with me. He nodded, still looking ahead, and commented that our situation didn't look good. My boat was less supportive of us as we neared the most violent part of the hole. His boat was thrown back at us; paddles were flying. A surge of water knocked us over. I came up panicked for the first time and grabbed a cockpit rim. Charlie appeared and stood motionless.

"I felt a rope under me and went under to unravel it. I tried to put the throw bag back in the boat and lost my stability. Boats and paddles went in different directions; I panicked again. I surfaced next to Charlie's Mirage II, and he came up next to my Mirage. I learned a lesson: hold onto the cockpit rim with both hands to conserve energy. Charlie mentioned that he was getting tangled in rope, so I offered my Tekna knife. He said he thought he could work free. He went under. When he came up, he appeared shaken and exhausted. He never spoke to me again; he simply stood, without a boat for stability.

"My morale was badly shaken by his silence; it was getting toward dusk. I could see people on the Illinois shore, three-quarters of a mile away, but I knew our plight had gone unnoticed. My warm-up pants were being pulled down. I knew I would drown if I didn't get them off. I attempted to hold the cockpit rim with one hand and free my legs. The pants ballooned full of water and dragged me under. I managed to get free and surface next to Charlie's boat. I returned to my strategy of conserving energy by holding on to the boat, but I was alarmed that the Mirage II's foam wall was working loose, along with the air bags. It was imperative to stand to conserve energy and not swallow water. The time was 5:35.

"Within minutes Charlie was pulled under. He did not resurface standing but floated on his back as he was dragged to the center of the hydraulic. He was recycled three times; he was not going to make it. I could see the ropes becoming tangled around his body in the deeper part of the hole where I dared not go.

"My thoughts turned to my own survival. I was afraid that I might no longer have enough energy to work my way out. I concentrated on careful, slow crabbing to the right. Several times I lost my footing. Suddenly, about five feet from the end of the hole, I popped free, along with Charlie's boat. It was now 5:40. I was too exhausted to hand paddle. I simply pulled myself up onto the boat and drifted slowly downstream towards the Missouri bank. I managed to reach the St. Louis water treatment plant and called police at 5:51. They were there within minutes. When we reached a view of the hole, neither Charlie nor the boat was in it. The police searched the shoreline; the Coast Guard boat arrived and spotted the body drifting in an eddy. Both safety ropes were wrapped around his body, and his PFD was only attached to one arm. Attempts to revive Charlie were in vain."

Although not as abrupt as the accident before this, the outcome here is, of course, just as final. Charlie Schulman will never boat again. For those of us who will, this accident clearly points out the danger of low dams and other steep-entry hydraulics. In particular, it highlights the danger of crossing the boil line of these holes and the need for absolute concentration when ferrying in the vicinity, leaving a margin for error if possible for surges in the current. If this hole had been too deep to stand in, neither man would have survived.

Difficult to remember though it is, the first duty of a rescuer is to himself or herself. Herm Smith risked his life to assist Charlie Schulman by getting into the hole beyond his limits when he could have escaped easily. A better approach (suggested later by Smith and seconded by the editors) would be to try to effect a rescue by throwing a rope from a nearby island. If that had failed, Smith could have paddled below the victim and thrown a rope across the boil line. By turning over and swamping his kayak, he might have then been able to use the current to pull his friend free. Obviously, the presence of other people would have greatly increased their margin for error and greatly simplified the rescue. However, their small group size was not unreasonable for the location and was emphatically not the cause of the accident.

The loose rope from a throw bag complicated the rescue. Proper rope storage is crucial for reducing the possibility of entanglement, but in a surf as long as this one it is impossible to guarantee that even a properly stored rope won't work loose. Although Charlie turned down the offer of a knife, one could have been useful to the victim and was certainly reassuring to the survivor. Charlie had just bought a knife, but he had not yet attached it to his life vest. Take the time needed to do these little jobs before your next trip. Also, be aware of variations in skill from day to day which all boaters experience. Charlie's off day may have led to the error that caused the accident and his inability to extricate himself; additionally, it is particularly important not to become complacent about paddling in areas you frequently run. Death can strike in a single moment of inattention, and even the best efforts of boating companions will sometimes fail to turn the blow.

When we look for reasons, explanations for accidents, we can often find them. Rash acts by novices result, sometimes, in disaster, and lapses of judgment or, to look at the choices another way, acts of bravado may well lead to disaster. Boaters who exhibit a pattern of subtle carelessness, a slightly too-casual approach to river safety, may, despite decades of river experience, eventually find their years of getting by halted abruptly. Solo boating, with its added dangers and reduced margin for error, can claim expert paddlers, leaving us to wonder whether the added pleasures of being on the river by oneself and the added convenience of going alone are worth the added risk. And two-boat parties, which for the advanced paddler usually mean two-person trips, although offering the boaters a wonderful opportunity to enjoy the river with one close friend, may not allow the single rescuer the range of options he or she might have otherwise. All of this is true. But truth should not lead us to finger-pointing. While it is true, for example, that a four-boat party is usually safer than a party of only two boats, people still die on four-boat trips, and many two-boat runs are perfectly successful.

5

The following accounts are notable because the most common risk factors, discussed in Chapter 1, are conspicuously absent. For the most part, the proper equipment is used, prudent safety precautions are taken, and reasonable judgment is exercised. While it is true that many of these accidents occur on difficult runs, in no case is the river obviously beyond the skill of the victim, although some boaters have invoked this argument as a reason for some of the accidents. And while it is possible in hindsight to suggest different choices the victims could have made, or different rescue options, it is not possible to say with certainty that the choices they made and the options tried were wrong. In their place, we might have done the same.

The first account, a 1991 report of a kayaker who drowned in June on the Little Susitna River near Hatcher Pass, Alaska, involves a party of only two, but because of the great difficulty of effecting a boat-based rescue in continuous big water, the scenario would most likely have played out to exactly the same grim conclusion even if more boaters had been on hand.

Tom McAssey

The Little Susitna River is a steep, boulder-choked class V run known for its continuous rapids and few large eddies. Like most Alaskan rivers, the Little Susitna's waters are frigid. The victim, Tom McAssey, was an experienced kayaker who had run the river between seventy and eighty times, including five or six times during the previous week, according to news reports. His partner was equally experienced. It is possible that a back injury Tom had suffered shortly before his death may have kept him from boating to capacity.

Tom was in Death Ferry rapid when he flipped. He recovered his equipment but slammed into downstream rocks. Dazed and unresponsive, he was unable to grab his partner's boat for rescue. His swim went on for miles. He was in the water for fifteen minutes, and after a while he began to float facedown. His partner, after making numerous attempts to effect a boat rescue, raced ahead to places where the current was slower and tried to pick Tom up. This did not work. Realizing that a construction crew would be working downstream at a bridge, the boater sprinted ahead. On the way, he was able to ask a motorist parked along the riverbank to call for help. By the time he got downstream, state police had been called. Working upstream, the group found Tom about 200 yards above the bridge. CPR was performed, but he could not be revived.

The simple truth is that rescuing an unconscious swimmer in fast-moving water is extremely difficult. The only option with a real chance for success is for a paddler to abandon his or her boat and to attempt a swimming rescue, bringing the victim in to shore, which is a very dangerous procedure on a river of this difficulty. With more back up it might have been tried in some of the slower spots, but the risk to the swimming rescuer would still have been extreme. Perhaps the reported back injury argued for Tom to have stayed off the river for a while, but several successful runs during the previous week suggest the back injury was not a serious impediment. In addition, it is unclear whether Tom's ignoring his equipment would have made a difference; he might have been better able to protect himself without having to worry about his boat and paddle.

Rivers of this difficulty carry with them considerable risk of death or injury, and Death Ferry is a serious drop. A missed roll can have consequences that can only be weighed beforehand, before committing to the run. The next accident also shows the results of a missed roll in difficult water. This time, a group of expert boaters is on hand, but they can give no assistance.

David Decot

On May 20, 1985, a group of expert kayakers scouted a steep and not commonly run section of the Merced River at El Portal, California. This is a stretch of continuous class V whitewater, and demanding rapids start immediately below the put-in. At the 2000-cfs level, the river is fast and cold, making the rescue of a swimmer extremely difficult. The drops are large, powerful, and complex, with many potential trouble spots and few places to recover. It is no place to have lapses in technique. David Decot, the victim, was skilled and competent, but he was the weakest paddler of the group. The run was certainly near the limits of his skill, but boaters generally improve by pushing their limits. However, the group had discussed the consequences of a swim, and David knew what he was getting into.

After arriving at the Chevron station south of El Portal, the group scouted the river. The spot where the accident occurred is behind a restaurant-motel complex, and the tree that caused the accident, a pine about two feet wide at the stump, was hidden from upstream inspection by a patio built out into the river. The tree itself was mostly underwater, giving few telltale signs to upstream viewers. This was the one spot on this stretch not scouted from the riverbank, primarily because the restaurant was built right up to the river and because it looked tame compared to the major part of the rapid, which lay upstream. The group launched their boats at an eddy at the top of the drop and moments later were committed to the run by a powerful current.

The first three boaters made the run without incident, although they clearly had their hands full. David flipped in the upper half of the drop, failed to roll, was carried helplessly into the half of the river blocked by the fallen pine, and disappeared without a trace. His boat remained near the surface, pinned against the tree. The accident was final and catastrophic; there was no way for the party to reach Dave or his boat to offer assistance.

A rescue squad was called, arriving in fifteen minutes—an excellent response time. At first, rescuers did not believe that the body was caught in the tree and suggested that the group search the shores downstream. After some discussion, they brought out their chain saw, a lightweight model in terrible condition with loose chain and dull teeth. It took almost twenty minutes to cut through the tree. Unfortunately, the tree wedged against a stump and held fast. They then sent someone out to get a bigger saw, which took about an hour. Once on the scene, the big saw cut through the trunk in less than a minute. When the tree was loose at last, boat and body floated free and were recovered downstream. By that time, of course, it was too late to do anything for David.

If the smaller saw had been in good condition, there is an outside chance that the group might have recovered Dave in time to resuscitate him. With the cold water reducing his oxygen demand, he might have survived, but Dave's age was working against him.

As the difficulty of a rapid increases, so does the penalty for error. Running class V+ drops demands unusual physical and mental fitness and is something that even skilled paddlers may prefer not to do. Those who do make such runs must realize the extent of their exposure to danger and make their judgments knowing that rescue is not, in many cases, a viable option. Additionally, the difficulty of jumping from one's car directly into class V+ rapids without a warm-up must not be underestimated. It is likely that this sudden transition worked against Dave, especially since the accident occurred early in the run. Boaters who enjoy these challenging runs need to keep in mind that special efforts must be made to warm up, especially on chilly days.

It is somewhat unusual for an expert paddler to die in technical whitewater. In fact, many experts die in rapids of less than class III. However, big drops are by definition extremely demanding, and rescue is difficult at best. Prevention, in the form of caution and good judgment, a willingness to bow out of a run that may be over one's head, is a paddler's best defense. However, since it is the nature of most boaters to push themselves, constantly seeking the challenge of more difficult water, bowing out of a run slightly harder than any they have run before may be difficult. Compounding the difficulty of the decision are subtle daily variations in skill, due to injury or other obvious factors or to something small, like too little sleep or how things are going at work. Perhaps some small and now forever unknown factor worked against Dane Wray on a late spring day in 1988 while boating in Idaho.

Dane Wray

The group in this account consisted of four kayakers. Mike, Ross, and Peter were British paddlers who were on a two-month tour of western rivers. The fourth, Dane Wray, a Canadian from Powell River, British Columbia, had joined the British boaters for a three-week vacation. All the kayakers had many years' experience paddling rivers of similar standard in North America and elsewhere; Dane, 36, had been kayaking since 1972 and had many exploratory first descents to his credit. He was one of the most experienced and respected kayakers in British Columbia. The river the group was running flows into the South Fork of the Salmon and has a reputation for being one of the best and most challenging kayak runs in Idaho. It drops at up to 180 feet per mile and in high water levels is a very continuous paddle, rated class IV-V, requiring complete commitment.

The group had spent the previous week paddling similar rivers in the area and were a happy and cohesive team with no problems or weaknesses. On the day of the accident, water levels were medium high, probably in the range of 1000 to 2000 cfs, giving powerful, continuous class IV+ water. The group set off and ran the first few miles or so with no problems—a challenging and enjoyable run. They made one portage around a log jam and immediately afterwards commenced paddling a section known as the Miracle Mile. Towards the end of this section is a class V rapid, some quarter of a mile long, which the group stopped to scout from the left bank. Mike and Ross successfully ran this rapid, choosing a line on river left and eddying out several times. They waited at the bottom for the other two.

Dane and Peter watched the first two run the rapid, and after a little deliberation, although portage was possible, both decided to run it. Dane led the way, missed a very tight eddy at the top, flipped, and was washed through two short falls and holes on the right of the river. He rolled up in an eddy behind a big boulder in the middle of the river. This experience must have shaken him, and we can imagine the talk he had with himself in the eddy, but he set off again, taking the main line down the center of the river. He successfully ran down most of the main section of the rapid, about 600 feet, but was flipped while entering the last major chute. He appeared to attempt to roll several times as he was washed down through some powerful hydraulics. At the end of the main chute he exited his kayak, after what appeared to be a struggle, and was last seen being washed down the next section of rapids around the corner.

Mike and Ross, on shore watching near the base of the rapid, were helpless in that Dane was out of reach of any throw line. Mike ran to his boat and set off in a nonstop pursuit down continuous class IV water. Meanwhile, Peter had run the main rapid on the left and set off after Mike to give assistance. Ross ran back to his boat and followed the other two down the river. The three kayakers paddled down the river separately looking for Dane but found no sign of him. Mike located Dane's boat and paddle some two miles down the river and about a mile farther pulled in. The others then caught up and decided that Mike and Ross would continue the river search down to the campsite while Peter walked back up a riverside trail in the hope that Dane had been washed ashore.

After reaching the campsite, Ross drove to the nearest town, twenty miles away by dirt road, to summon the Search and Rescue Team. Mike ran back and joined Peter at the scene of the accident. The two then began a thorough check of the river and banks downstream from the accident site. They spotted Dane's body against the far bank, a rock face, about a quarter of a mile from where he was last seen. There was no way across the river, and it was now 7:00 P.M., some three hours after the accident. Peter and Mike returned to the campsite, broke the news to Ross, and then met the sheriff and the local Search and Rescue Team. The sheriff decided to recover the body the following morning.

The next day the Search and Rescue Team organized the recovery of Dane's body. The group—sheriff, Search and Rescue Team, local river runners, two horses, and kayaks—set off at 10:00 A.M. up the narrow trail to the scene of the accident.

The three kayakers ferried across the river and climbed around to where Dane was. He was pinned underwater, with his legs and lower body trapped between a log and a slippery rock ledge that sloped down into the river, almost in reach from the bank but in a difficult spot above a falls. Belayed by the others, Mike eventually managed to get a line around the body, but it was pinned so securely that repeated efforts by the three could not pull it out. A chain saw was used to cut through the end of the log that was jammed against the rock face, unpinning the body by dislodging the log. Dane's body was recovered, ferried across the river, and carried on horseback down to the campsite, where it was entrusted to the local coroner at about 4:00 P.M.

This unfortunate incident points out that backup is difficult in serious whitewater. A safety boat in the water might have allowed for rescue if the victim could have been reached before he lost consciousness, but given the continuous nature of the whitewater downstream and the difficulty of towing someone to shore, success would have been far from certain. Also, unconsciousness may overtake a swimmer with surprising speed, as the next accident shows.

Mel Zajak

On Sunday, July 13, 1986, Mel Zajak and his group were boating in Chilliwack Canyon, a class IV run near Vancouver, Canada. Mel, 30, was a strong intermediate paddler with a very reliable roll. He had numerous class IV runs under his belt and was virtually never known to swim. Fully aware of the canyon's dangers and routes, he put in that morning with Mark, Graeme, and John soon after another group had started down the river. The river was 1.5-1.6 on the cable-pool gauge, an optimal level for the run.

When Mel's party reached the long rapid just above the cable-pool gauge, they eddied out on river left, as usual. Immediately below this eddy is a treacherous, weirlike hole that extends twenty feet from the left shore. To the rapid's far right is a serious string of holes and boulders that threaten pinning, wrapping, or boat breaking. The usual route is to swing out of the river-left eddy—above the keeper—to a five-foot center tongue, then immediately ferry left to avoid another major hole fifteen feet downstream. After a long S-turn requiring much rock dodging and either avoiding or punching, at this level, a wide hole at the bottom, paddlers eddy out next to the gauge. The rapid is a good quarter-mile long.

Mel was the last to leave the eddy. About the time he exited it, John back-endered and rolled in a hole below, temporarily diverting the group's attention. When Mark looked back upstream, he saw Mel's paddle flashing vertically in the weirlike keeper. Perhaps Mel was attempting to work his way out of the hole; no one will ever know how he got there in the first place. Mark immediately parked his kayak and began bushwhacking his way upstream with a throw rope in hand. Shortly before he reached the hole, he glimpsed Mel's boat sideways in it, but no sign of Mel. His next glimpse through the trees was of Mel floating facedown six feet downstream of the hole. Graeme paddled next to the body most of the way down the rapid; there was nothing he could do to rescue Mel until they reached a pool.

Meanwhile, the earlier group of kayakers had eddied out at the gauge below. They saw the paddle and boat come by, then Mel's body, still facedown. Steve C. and Steve W. rushed to Mel, removed his helmet, heaved his body onto the bow of a kayak, and attempted mouth-to-mouth. Mel's lungs were so full of water that mouth-to-mouth produced only a gurgle. Because he was extremely heavy and because they were drifting into the next rapid, very little more could have been done had a raft not passed by at that point and dragged the body aboard. The guide began CPR even before hitting an eddy below, where two doctors on the trip joined in the resuscitation efforts. They picked Mel up by his heels to empty water from his lungs and, with trained members of the group, continued CPR for nearly two hours. Other paddlers rounded up some fishermen to speed them to a telephone.

Rescuers never got a pulse from Mel, even from the beginning. His eyes were dilated, and his lips were blue from the time he floated into the gauge eddy. Mark estimated that Mel was recirculated in the upper hole for about two minutes—no one will ever know how much of that time he was unconscious—and that it took at least another two minutes for his body to reach the paddlers one-quarter mile below. When the ambulance arrived along a gravel road that cuts in to the river at that point, the crew administered adrenaline and oxygen and used the defibrillator, all without success. Mel was pronounced dead. The coroner arrived a few hours later.

Mel was wearing a wet suit, a life jacket, and a good helmet, but the autopsy revealed soft tissue damage on the back of the head. The coroner says the impact would not have been strong enough to knock him unconscious for long, but it may have shaken him up enough for him to inhale some water.

Twenty-six paddlers attended his funeral, a strong show of respect and concern. Following the funeral, many of these paddlers gathered to discuss what measures might be taken to prevent future tragedies. A number of suggestions were made, including cutting a trail around the rapid to make portage an easier option. In general, the conclusion was that many paddlers had become too complacent on the river, taking the attitude of "it won't happen to me." Many emphasized the need to watch out for one another more carefully.

Boaters who filed a report of Mel's accident said, in part, "It is the hope of all paddlers who were involved with this incident, and those who knew Mel, that this tragedy not be brushed off and forgotten soon. It's a reminder to us that our sport involves risk—of death as well as injury—to all, regardless of skill level. Already we've heard two paddlers comment, 'He shouldn't have been on the river.' This is disturbing in that the message is, 'I'm above that happening to me,' which is true for no paddler. And it's callous to those still saddened by this tragedy."

Although it is easy to say that all boaters should be allowed to decide what rivers they should be on, it is also easy, despite the above warning, to pass judgment on a boater's skill and experience and say, "He shouldn't have been there" when faced with an accident that is otherwise difficult to explain. The following accident has had this same criticism leveled against it.

Shawn Smith

Dr. Shawn Smith of Santa Rosa, California, drowned while kayaking on the Eel River on Wednesday, November 28, 1984. Shawn was a practicing physician, age 33, in excellent physical condition. His skill level was advanced (class IV), and he had recently made a fine run through Clavey Falls on the Tuolumne River, at about 5000 cfs. Although he had been paddling for five years, his experience level was not extensive, particularly when it came to reading turbulent, muddy water under high flow conditions. However, the summer before, he had completed an extended tour of Idaho that undoubtedly improved his skill and added to his experience. His accident occurred on the popular Pillsbury run during high water, when heavy fall rains had filled Lake Pillsbury, spilling over the top of Scott Dam (3100 cfs from the dam, 5300 cfs at the take-out). His paddling companions that Wednesday, Bill Senerchia and Dan Wineberg, were not experienced and in fact had not done the Pillsbury run before, at any water level.

The Pillsbury run is intermediate in difficulty, usually considered class III. It is commonly run in the summer, with a hydro release of 350 cfs, and in the winter and early spring at a typical flow of 500 to 1500 cfs. Only when Lake Pillsbury is full and a major storm occurs does the flow exceed this range, and then the difficulty increases by a full grade to class IV.

The accident occurred in the runout for a rapid called Dennis's Menace, the most difficult on the run, about three miles below Scott Dam. This rapid changes dramatically at higher flows, and Shawn had seen it previously only at lower water levels. At summer flows, a large boulder blocks almost the whole channel, leaving only a constricted jet which doglegs off the rock wall on river left. At moderate flows—1000 cfs—the dogleg chute becomes more turbulent, but a sneak chute opens up on the right. At higher flows, water pours over the boulder and creates a large hole that routinely flips and recirculates rafts. The right-side route becomes the preferred choice, but its approach is guarded by a row of boulders extending from the right bank. At moderate flows, a boat can sneak between the boulders, but at higher flows, the boulders create hydraulics that merge and form a wide hole offset from the large hydraulic just downstream on river left. These large holes can be skirted by experienced paddlers, but a strong, committed move is required.

The run begins easily, and about three miles below Scott Dam slides on the right mark the beginning of a series of rapids that culminate in Dennis's Menace. High water often changes perspective, and Shawn may not have recognized the rapid. However, he did eddy out in the pool on the right, just above Dennis's Menace. Wineberg joined him in the eddy, but Senerchia didn't try for the eddy and dropped into the large hole. He flipped, washed out, and rolled up downstream. Wineberg followed, was tumbled by the hole, and swam out. Shawn followed and presumably went into the hole, too. When he failed to join his companions downstream, they walked back upstream and found him trapped in his boat, broached on a snag. He was still conscious, but only with tremendous effort could he hold his head above water. Both his legs were broken. A rope was thrown to Shawn, who was about fifteen feet from shore, but he could not hold on and expired soon after. His body was recovered the next day, when the water had subsided substantially.

The snag itself was the stub of a branch, about three inches in diameter, from a fallen oak tree that had its roots well above water on the left bank, a steep landslide slope just downstream of the rock wall at Dennis's Menace. The top of the tree leaned down into the water, and the branch stuck vertically above the surface, leaning slightly upstream. At lower flows, the water forms a gentle eddy here, but at higher flows, the eddy washes out. Only six inches of the branch stub were showing.

Since Wineberg and Senerchia were far downstream, preoccupied with Wineberg's swim, the following reconstruction of the wrap is partly speculative: Shawn dropped into the hole and washed out, but he was shoved left instead of down the center as his companions were. He may have flipped and rolled so that he did not have time to see the snag, but it would have been difficult to see anyway since it only stuck six inches above the muddy water. If he had seen it soon enough, it would have been easy to avoid, but he did not. His boat floated upright and sideways into the snag, hitting it exactly at the midpoint, so that his boat did not pivot off. Instead, the soft plastic of the boat probably dented upon impact, leading to two consequences: first, the dent gripped the obstacle, preventing the boat from slipping off; second, the dent initiated the collapse of the cockpit between the pillars, pinning Shawn immediately. The slight upstream lean of the snag forced the boat downward, rather than up and over.

The hazard of soft, rotomolded polyethylene kayaks is well known. Their tendency to fold instead of pivot off, coupled with their subsequent failure to break apart, makes them dangerous. Many new boats are a substantial improvement, with the impressive rigidity of blow-molded, high density polyethylene, and larger cockpits. However, a few old boats are still in use and should be considered hazardous. Although even a more rigid boat might have failed in this situation, any increase in the potential time for escape could save lives. But, it is important to note that the increasingly smaller size and tighter fit of many new designs counter, to a degree, the improved safety of larger cockpits and stiffer material. A point to remember when trading off the ease of exiting a larger boat for performance is that although the river is usually forgiving, it sometimes isn't.

Some observers have questioned the wisdom of this high-water run. While high water is very exciting, it can of course be difficult to read and intolerant of error. Sometimes paddlers make high-water runs like this because of confidence in their bomb-proof rolls, but the ability to roll will not always get one out of trouble. Whether it was wise to make this high-water run or not, perhaps Shawn should have shore-scouted the drop. However, the shore-scout may not have forewarned him of the snag, which was barely visible, about seventy-five feet downstream of the hole, and appeared rather inocuous. Nevertheless, a shore-scout would at least have revealed the offset lineup and the severity of the holes. After all, Shawn did eddy out, following only after Senerchia blew by and flushed through the drop.

Little is known about the attempts at rescue in this accident. The group had a rope and was reasonably prepared. But what was their rescue training? Although in this case the shock and massive internal bleeding resulting from the broken femurs made the victim less able to take part in efforts toward his own rescue than he might have been otherwise, even an uninjured but trapped boater is largely at the mercy of his or her paddling partners. A heads-up pin, where the victim can breathe, although sometimes only with great effort, affords valuable time to organize an effective rescue. In the following account, a group of paddlers, with help from other parties on the river, nearly succeed in rescuing their pinned friend.

Glenn Clark

At approximately 10:30 on the morning of January 25, 1987, a group of six kayakers, including Glenn Clark, put in on the Mulberry Fork of the Warrior River, near Garden City, Alabama, for a day of whitewater paddling. As on many winter days in the Southeast, there was a light rain falling, and the air temperature was in the low 40s. The water temperature was slightly colder than this, but all of the paddlers were adequately dressed for these weather conditions by wearing either wet suits or dry suits.

The river gauge at the put-in was reading 3.8 feet and rising. At this level most of the rocks are submerged, and the rapids consist mainly of a series of holes and waves. High water made the river very silty, and it was impossible to see anything under the surface. Even considering the cold, the difficulty of the run was within the group's ability. All members were experienced kayakers who had paddled rivers that are bigger and technically more difficult than the Mulberry. Additionally, all of the paddlers had frequently paddled the river and knew it very well.

It was approximately 11:00 A.M. when the group arrived at the second rapid on the river, a straightforward run generally regarded as a class II+ or III. At this level, the only large rock in the rapid forms a hole that can provide pop-ups. The problem with this play spot is the existence of a tree stump about seventy feet directly downstream in the middle of the main current. Water just barely forms a pillow over the top of the stump at this level, making it difficult to see it from upstream among the standing waves. However, because of the group's knowledge, the stump was not a hidden danger. In fact, several paddlers in the group commented to one another on the need to be careful of it.

The group stopped to play for about ten minutes until one of the paddlers mentioned he was heading on downstream. He was followed by three of the other paddlers. Glenn and the last other paddler were still in the eddy on river right when Glenn asked, "Are you going?" The other paddler said yes and peeled out to head downstream, leaving Glenn alone in the eddy. Several seconds later the boaters heard yells for help. Glenn's boat was broached on the stump at the bottom of the rapid.

Because of the location of the stump, it is the group's opinion that Glenn had gone out to play in the hole one last time before heading downstream. The kayak, a Perception Dancer, was broached with the long axis of the boat almost perpendicular to the current, the bow just slightly downstream of the stern, facing river right. The boat was turned on its side just over 90 degrees, with the cockpit facing downstream. The stump was across the top part of Glenn's upper thighs, with his torso river left of the stump. The right cockpit rim was visible, pressed against the stump about one inch below the top. Most of the rest of the stump and the boat were hidden under the silty water.

Members of the paddling group were able to reach Glenn by paddling into the surface eddy created by his boat. It was all Glenn could do to help hold his head above water, and there was no way Glenn could try to free himself. He was panicky and only said that he was hung; he did not say how. But it was obvious that the boat was pinned solidly on the stump. His friends tried to calm Glenn by talking with him while supporting his body and keeping his head above water.

Some members of the group tried getting out of their boats and into the water to help free Glenn's boat. But the water was chest deep and the current was strong, and it was very difficult to stay with him. However, there were usually two people in the water with Glenn at all times; one would support Glenn while the other tried to free him. It was extremely difficult not to be swept away by the current. In fact, as they tried to free Glenn, they were all eventually swept downstream. But whenever they were swept away, they would immediately try to paddle or swim back to him.

The group attempted to free Glenn in a variety of ways. They were able to pull the stern of his boat about 30 degrees downstream, but it would not come off. Even the full weight of a rescuer holding onto the rear grab loop and letting the current pull him downstream failed to free it. The group also tried lifting the boat over the stump, but to no avail. The force of the current made pushing the boat upstream out of the question.

The top of the stump comes to a somewhat blunt point only a couple of inches in diameter, making standing on the stump to assist Glenn impossible. Since the stump was pressed directly against Glenn and his boat, it was also impossible to hold onto the stump or to tie anything off to it. It was deemed too dangerous to try to get to the upstream side of the boat or to climb onto the boat itself. Either of these methods could have made the situation worse by trapping another person or by pushing Glenn's boat underwater.

It became clear that getting a rope to Glenn's boat was necessary. From the nearest eddy, upstream and to river left, rescuers tried to throw a rope to the boat but were unsuccessful. The strong current, the waist-deep water in the eddy, saplings in the way, the distance between the boat and the rescuers, and the pillow of water formed by Glenn's boat combined to thwart their efforts. Next they tried to ferry the rope across to Glenn, but because of the current and the distance, this was also unsuccessful. The plan was to attach the rope to the stern grab loop and to pull the boat off to river left. The rescuers felt sure this would be successful once they got a rope attached to Glenn's boat.

One member of the group left to try to find help. By this time Glenn had been pinned for about twenty-five minutes and was barely able to hold himself out of the water.

Three more boaters arrived at this time. They worked with the paddlers who were already there, and attempts were made to ferry another slightly longer rope across and to throw this rope, but these efforts met with the same results. The position of the pin right in the center of the main flow made access very difficult. The cold, rising water was now coming completely over Glenn's boat, and he was drifting in and out of consciousness; soon he lost consciousness for the last time.

Another paddling group arrived with a still longer rope, and they joined in attempting to get to Glenn's boat to assist in holding him up. This was also the first group with an open canoe. The open canoe was able to ferry the longer rope from river left to the eddy below Glenn's boat. Because of the rising water, it was now impossible for the people in the water to get to the stern grab loop, although attempts were made to hook the rope to the stern grab loop by paddling to the stern of Glenn's boat and reaching underwater for the loop. When these efforts failed, the rope was put around Glenn's waist with a butterfly knot and carabiner so that it wouldn't bind on his body. Several paddlers pulled the rope from river left at various angles to try to free the boat, but the boat still would not come off. The county sheriff, rescue squads, and fire departments had reached the scene by now, but the location made it impossible to get a vehicle or motorboat near the river.

As the water was still rising and the cold was taking its toll on the rescuers, it was becoming increasingly difficult to stay with Glenn and hold his head above the water. Eventually all the rescuers were washed downstream. As there was now no one with Glenn and he was unconscious, his head dropped into the water. The time was noted at 12:29 P.M. A number of paddlers tried again to get in the water with Glenn. Most got washed downstream immediately, but a couple were able to get to Glenn for just a few moments; as soon as they tried to raise Glenn's head or free the boat, however, they were swept downstream as well.

Some paddlers continued to try to reach Glenn, and others tied three of the rescue squad's ropes together to set up a Telfer lower, a system using several ropes to lower boats to a pinned victim. This technique takes time to set up, and the attempt was not possible until the rescue squad arrived with enough rope. The plan was to lower several boats, tied together for stability, to the pinned kayak and to attach a rope to the stern grab loop. However, the nose of the canoe kept diving underwater whenever rescuers leaned down to attach the rope. After several attempts, the boats were forced back to shore because the canoe was filling up with water.

Because the water was rising, or perhaps because Glenn's boat was shifting on the stump, the ends of the broached boat now began pivoting in and out of the water by about one or two feet. The canoe was disconnected from the Telfer lower and was paddled out to the pinned boat, with one paddler lying across the bow of the canoe with another rope. Since the stern grab loop was now bouncing in and out of the water, the plan was to hook the rope to the loop while it was out of the water, a variation of the earlier attempt. The rescuers felt that this might now work since the grab loop was not continuously underwater as it had been earlier. After several tries, the boater was able to hook the stern grab loop as it bounced up out of the water. This rope was ferried to river left and tied to the big ropes used for the Telfer lower. About ten to fifteen people on river right then pulled on the ropes from about 100 to 150 feet upstream, at about an eleven-o'clock angle from the broached boat, looking down from above. The boat came off the stump and was pulled to river right. The time was noted as 1:55 P.M.

One of the paddlers started CPR immediately, assisted by members of the rescue squad. After about five minutes, the county coroner and a doctor who was present pronounced Glenn dead at the scene. Glenn had been pinned for about two hours and forty-five minutes and had been underwater for almost an hour and a half. Even though Glenn was pinned for a long time, some rescuers continued efforts in the hope that he could be revived due to the cold water's lowering his metabolic rate. This was not the case, however. Two of the paddlers were taken away by the rescue squad and treated for hypothermia.

Clearly this was a difficult and unusual pinning. The boat did not fold, collapse, or otherwise fail and was not at fault; the problem was that the stump blocked the cockpit opening, preventing the paddler's escape. When swimming rescues did not work, the rope rescue became the only alternative. In each of the first three paddling groups to arrive, there were people with formal rescue and whitewater instructor training. All the groups had throw ropes, carabiners, prusik loops, and knives. But although a lot of competent people were on the scene, the rescue seemed to lack coordination. An obvious question is why, if one rope could not reach, several ropes were not clipped or tied together. Perhaps the cold and the pressures of the moment clouded the judgment of those involved and the presence of paddlers from several trips made coordinated activities difficult.

Although offered in hindsight, one technique that might have helped was to hook a carabiner through a sling and then over the cockpit rim or else to wrap a prusik around the stump below the kayak. Either method could have provided a firm hold for rescuers at the center of the boat, and from this position they possibly could have worked their way to the grab loops, which, once attached to a rope, would have anchored the lifesaving pull. Broach loops, like those on many contemporary boats, would have provided both an anchor for rescuers and an attachment point for a rope from shore. Also, a saw might have allowed the rescuers to cut the stump and free the boat.

It is in fact all too easy for us as boaters upon reading this account to come up with a number of rescue techniques that we would have tried if only we had been there. After all, according to the report, Glenn was pinned heads-up for more than an hour and fifteen minutes. Surely, we might think, given that much time, there must have been a way to save the fellow. Yes, the people on the scene tried hard, tried heroically, but we could, well, we could . . . As much as we might wish that we had been there on the Mulberry to help Glenn Clark during his long pin, let us hope that we are never in such a situation on one of our own trips, with one of our own friends. If so, let us hope our rescue efforts succeed. The long, inexorable death of a close friend, despite our best efforts at rescue, and the lifetime to think about what else we might have done would be terribly hard to deal with.

Of course, a quick death in a heads-down pin is also horrifying.

Steve Schaub

Flowing near Marble, Colorado, upstream of the Redstone Bridge, the Crystal River is a fast, technical mountain stream providing plenty of class IV action in a very narrow streambed. The group on the river the day of this accident consisted of five advanced to expert boaters: Steve Schaub, Roger Belston, M.D., Jim Sindelar, and Jim's two college-aged sons, Charles and Joel. They had met at the Arkansas two days earlier and had relocated to other rivers because of high water. Arriving at Bogen Flat campground in the morning, they spent the rest of the day scouting and sightseeing around Marble. Steve and Roger had boated the river the week before at higher water, but none of the others had seen it before.

Steve Schaub, the victim, was 50 years old, but he looked much younger and was in excellent physical condition. He had been kayaking for twenty-five years, with many trips to Colorado, Idaho, Newfoundland, and elsewhere. He was an excellent swimmer, very much at home in the water, and he rarely got into trouble. If he swam, he usually rescued himself and his gear faster than others could get to him. He was wearing good equipment, including a Farmer John wet suit, helmet, and life jacket. His boat was an epoxy Lettman racing kayak.

Jim Sindelar recounts the accident:

"The morning of June 10, 1990, dawned gray and rainy, so the group got a leisurely start, putting in below Marble in the early afternoon with plans to run down to the Redstone Bridge. We looked very carefully beforehand at the two so-called culverts. Doug Wheat's *Floater's Guide to Colorado* recommends portaging them, but they are often run by kayakers. Indeed, Roger Belston had run them on a previous trip. The culverts are actually three twelve-foot-wide rectangular concrete tunnels that carry the river underneath County Road 314. To an approaching boater, they look like the letter E with legs down and the road across the backbone. The concrete dividers are about ten inches wide, with sharp, square corners. The headroom obviously depends on the water level.

"We scouted these culverts, looking carefully for logs or other obstructions, but found all tunnels clean. The first culvert was no problem: the current approached in line, and there was about four feet of headroom. We had all planned to run it and did so without difficulty. The second was another matter. Here, the river, after running along the left side of the road, makes an abrupt 90-degree bend, immediately entering the culvert tunnels. The current was strong and tricky, and headroom was just barely enough for a kayaker if he ducked a little. The currents boiled and surged, with a lot of water going to the outside of the turn. Roger, who had run it before, suggested that the inside tunnel was the best bet because the currents are less turbulent there. I thought it looked nasty and said so but made no decision until the day we made the run.

"As our group approached the second culvert, my sons and I decided to portage. Roger, with Steve close behind, dropped around the corner towards the culverts. I carried my boat across the road to see Roger downstream in his boat—he yelled that Steve was stuck. I ran across to the upstream face to see the shadow of Steve's kayak, completely underwater by at least six inches, wrapped around the divider between the right and center tunnel. The boat had broached, tipped upstream, wrapped just forward of the cockpit, and collapsed on Steve's legs. The bow of the boat was in the tunnel on river right. The stern and Steve's body trailed downstream into the center tunnel. His head was under about two feet of water, with the full force of the current hitting him in the chest and face.

"As I approached, Steve raised his right hand, clearing the water surface by about eight inches. This was about six feet below the narrow, sloping shoulder where I was standing. I removed my rescue-belt-cum-carabiner, flopped onto my belly, and, with the help of the others who held my legs, managed to put the webbing in his hand. Steve got both hands on the webbing and could apply his full strength to it. He could not work clear of the boat or raise his head to breathe. I saw a flash of helmet break the surface just once and speculate that this was when he cleared the one leg that I later learned he worked free. We fought this way for five to six minutes, straight pulls, surges. At times it seemed we were gaining, but in retrospect we probably pulled his body towards the surface only to lose ground again. There was no real chance of pulling the boat free or getting Steve's head above the surface to breathe. Once he lost the webbing, but he stuck his hands up again and we started anew.

"After about six minutes the webbing went slack, and it was apparent that Steve had lost consciousness. I tied onto a rescue rope and, belayed by others, went down over the edge. Bracing on the concrete and the submerged boat I tried blocking the current, pulling on the life jacket, tugging on the loose leg I eventually found, but accomplished nothing. By this time some cars had stopped and someone suggested tying a rope to the loose leg and pulling with a car. This last desperate effort on our part broke the quarter-inch rescue rope. At this point, about fifteen minutes after the accident, the Carbondale Rescue Squad pulled up. Completely exhausted, I asked to be pulled up to make way for fresh men, including a swift-water rescue specialist who directed efforts from then on.

"After approximately forty-five minutes the Carbondale Rescue Squad freed the kayak. They worked a heavy rope around the bow of Steve's boat using a twenty-foot pole, then maneuvered their truck upstream of the bridge hard against a cliff and set up a double or triple Z-drag. Boat and boater were released, washing through the tunnel to be recovered by swimmers below. CPR and the best efforts of Glenwood Springs Hospital were to no avail. There was no water in Steve's lungs; he simply asphyxiated."

Steve Schaub was a responsible and careful boater. He had scouted the culvert, was not afraid to portage, and would not have attempted the drop unless he believed himself capable of running it. No one saw the wrap, but Jim's best guess is that Steve spun out in a small eddy on river right. Unable to gain control quickly enough, he broached right in the cockpit area. Had the boat not collapsed, he would have swum, and maybe lost his boat, considered it a screwup, but nothing more.

The boat was built with a wall in front of the feet but not between the feet and the front of the cockpit. Modern boats are typically made with full walls and a larger cockpit, which might have made a difference. While on the topic of equipment, it is worth noting that the breaking of the quarter-inch rescue line suggests that lightweight polypropylene marine line of this thickness, found in some compact rescue bags, is a poor compromise between strength and weight.

Unlike the situation in the previous account, access to this pin site was relatively easy. It is hard to imagine a quicker response to this pinning. Help was on hand instantly, contact was made, and the rescuers kept trying new approaches and did not give up until exhausted. In the light of living-room hindsight, it seems that this situation was made to order for a tag line. The river was narrow, the bridge provided quick access to both shores, and they had the rope and people to do it. Because the force of the water was great and Steve was pinned well below the surface, there were no guarantees, but if you are faced with similar circumstances, this approach is probably worth a try.

Little, in fact, is guaranteed in pins or broaches, except that the situation is deadly serious. The victim, of course, faces terrible danger, and often the rescuers do, too. The following account shows the risk to both.

Bob O'Connor

In the fall of 1982, a group of Georgia Tech Outdoor Program students entered Initiation Rapid, the Gauley's first major drop below Summersville Dam. This river is considered one of the most challenging big-water runs in the East, with numerous Class IV-V drops along its course. A flow of 2500 cfs, normal during the fall drawdown season, is considered optimal for safety and enjoyment, and the river was running at nearly that on September 24, the day of the accident. The Gauley's major rapids are powerful and occasionally intricate, with big drops separated by long pools. Invisible undercutting of several of the huge boulders adds to the river's risk. Bob O'Connor, recently appointed director of outdoor programs at Georgia Tech, had numerous runs of the Gauley to his credit and was fully prepared for the trip.

After warming up below the dam and downstream through minor rapids, the group headed off into Initiation Rapid. Initiation's top half is fairly easy, and the bottom half is a sliding ledge dropping eight feet in about thirty yards. Most paddlers that day ran the center route without incident.

O'Connor was traveling midgroup. Whether he voluntarily chose to run right or was pushed by an unexpected current is unknown. In any case, as he neared a big, sloping boulder on the right, Bob washed up against its shallow pillow of water, expecting to bank off it and slide into the pool below. Instead, his stern was sucked down into a crack between a dry rock on the right and the wet rock that made up part of the ledge. The crack narrows on the downstream end, and a basketball-sized rock is wedged there. His kayak pinned on this rock with the stern below the current and the bow pointed skyward at 50 degrees.

Seeing Bob's horrifying predicament, the group responded quickly. Henry DeGrazia reached the rock behind the pinned boat, but others had considerable difficulty crossing the tricky currents. Henry talked to Bob, who was trapped in the kayak with his head above water. They decided that Henry would give Bob one end of a rescue line and belay the other end on the rock. Bob and Henry pulled, attempting to give Bob the needed leverage to work free. Initially this seemed to be working, but at the last moment, the kayak pivoted 90 degrees. Later observation suggested that the boat's stern had initially rested on a small ledge, but then it fell off as the craft spun, plunging Bob deeper into the crack below.

The victim's plight worsened, and Henry called urgently for help. Others were trying to cross the current to the rock and reach the accident site but were unsuccessful. Two of the group walked upstream and began swimming toward the site, but only Dave Montanye made it to the rock. Belayed by Henry, Dave held one end of the rope and was able to reach Bob. By now the victim was pinned under a sheet of water, his head diverting the current to form an air pocket. He could talk but not move. Worse, he seemed gradually to be slipping down into the crack.

Dave grabbed Bob's life vest, then later, his arms. The jacket appeared to be caught on the rock and rode higher as the victim slipped down. The air pocket, moreover, was shrinking fast. Dave pulled on Bob's arms with all his strength—one arm tugging at Bob, the other holding the belay line—but nothing could break him from the grip of the current. As Dave became exhausted, the two rescuers changed places.

At this point kayaker Frannie Strickland arrived on the scene. She told the men of a similar incident on this spot several years earlier and that there was a tunnel under the rocks right there. The previous victim had passed through the tunnel and had come out downstream. Since the situation was becoming desperate, Henry took the risky step of reaching out over the victim and moving his boat so that Bob could wiggle free and go through the tunnel. The boat shifted, and both victim and rescuer plunged underwater. Bob's life jacket and Henry surfaced downstream, but there was no sign of Bob. Concerned that the boat might still be blocking Bob's passage, Dave worked his way out to the kayak and tried to move it. He lost his footing and also went safely through the tunnel.

Others, including Wick Walker and Dean Tomko, now mounted the rock. Wick, an expert boater stationed in Europe with the army, donned a German water-rescue harness and clipped onto Dean's rescue line. After probing the crack, Wick clipped a second line to the bow of Bob's boat and tried to pull it free. The boat shifted and sank. When they cut it loose, the boat floated free, but there was still no sign of Bob.

Earlier on, a runner had been sent to the dam, a mile upstream over rugged terrain. The water level began to drop soon after Wick's arrival. Wick again lowered himself into the crack. The walls widened into an underwater cavern that contained no snags or sign of the victim. Finally, a search party was formed which found Bob's body at the base of the drop. Many other boaters, trapped by the falling water level, spent the night in the canyon.

The Georgia Tech group did everything possible to mobilize an effective rescue. They were simply hampered by limited access to the site. The rescue attempt was more than competent—it was courageous. Henry DeGrazia and Dave Montanye both risked death by swimming through the crack that claimed Bob O'Connor's life. In this light, hindsight seems a disservice to their efforts, but it may help to check other possible options for similar situations.

When a victim is pinned in a heads-up, stable position, his or her condition will probably not deteriorate until rescue begins, and a brief delay to gather rescue forces is often advisable. Shortage of manpower at the site was the biggest problem in the O'Connor rescue attempt. Of course, decisions to delay should be made in consultation with the victim, since the situation could deteriorate. In any event, once the boat shifted, Bob's plight became desperate. One thing not tried was tying a rope to him, allowing a pull from solid footing. This might have pulled him free or allowed time to discover how he was trapped in the cockpit.

This incident shows the importance of having a well thought out plan before disturbing a pinned, stable paddler. But any strategy must be modified to meet the circumstances. In this case, the rescuers followed the victim's wishes. As Frannie Strickland said, people have survived swims through this tunnel, although deciding to swim here is taking a perilous option since debris may block the passage. Given the circumstances, it was a reasonable choice. Bob knew the risk. Had he not lost his life vest, a high-quality, well-fitting model, he might have survived the suckhole swim. This death shows that the most-competent and best-equipped people cannot guarantee rescue.

In the next account, telling of a pin on the New River in West Virginia, the situation is more confusing and access to the pin site is even more difficult. Boaters try for some time to effect a rescue.

Joe Fleming

On June 29, 1985, a group of veteran and intermediate kayakers put in at the Cunard Access to the New River. It was warm and sunny, with no need for wet suits or paddling jackets. The water temperature was about 70 degrees. After some warm-up, including pop-ups and rolls, the group of seven boaters headed downstream.

Below the landmark railroad trestle, about two miles downstream from Cunard, lies a large pool that leads to Lower Railroad Rapid. Scouting can be done from river left. At negative gauge levels, evidence of a broken ledge can be seen slightly right of center in the main wave train. Freezing during low winter flow caused a section of rock to break loose from the ledge and lodge slightly downstream, allowing some volume of water to pass under it. At normal levels this site offers little trouble and is a relatively easy class III+ drop. However, low water increases the hazard dramatically as a higher percentage of water goes under the rock. Low-water incidents here in the past, experienced by both commercial and private boaters, have resulted in destroyed or unrecovered equipment.

The river is rarely low enough to expose the rock, so prior knowledge and an experienced eye are essential to planning a safe low-water route. A sneak route exists to the right side but is abusive to boat and paddle. Most paddlers choose a line left of center, moving quickly to the left. The water level that day, -1.75 feet at the Fayette Station bridge gauge, left two to four inches of water going over the broken ledge.

Joe Fleming, 29, was a part-time guide on the Lehigh River, as were four others accompanying him. He was an intermediate kayaker capable of rolling. Two of the seven paddling together that day were veterans of many years of boating and had been on the New before at various levels, including low water.

The person most acquainted with this drop described it to the group, warning of the pin possibility, and set the correct line to follow. The first boaters had clean, uneventful runs. Joe was the sixth of seven to run, and he drifted too far right, with the last boater following. After bumping a few rocks, Joe's boat lodged on the upstream side of the undercut, with the last boater passing to the right. Joe's kayak pinned almost vertically, the exposed end pointing up and toward river right. Water was breaking over his head, forming an air pocket that allowed him to breathe. He could extend his hand free of the water, which he did, waving frantically. He remained in this semistable condition for ten to twelve minutes, while the current thwarted several efforts to reach the site. Three times rescuers threw a rope from river right into his waving hand, but he could not hold on.

At approximately 12:15 P.M., a New River Adventures trip arrived and radioed for help. About this time, the pinned kayak shifted, no longer allowing an air pocket to form, and detectable movement stopped. Mike Burns, one of the group of boaters, finally reached the rock by jumping from a raft that was ferried near. He tied the rope from river right to the exposed grab loop, and three people pulling hard managed to free the kayak. Joe was immediately pulled from his boat, and CPR began on the deck of a kayak. Joe was moved to the shore. Total rescue time was twenty to twenty-five minutes.

At a crucial time, help, even of a minor nature, may spell the difference between rescue and tragedy...

Four two-man teams were organized to perform CPR. At approximately 1:40 P.M. the National Park Service and paramedics arrived. Antiarrhythmic drugs were administered, and Joe was defibrillated. CPR was continued during evacuation until arrival at Plateau Medical Center at 3:46 P.M., where Joe was pronounced dead at 3:55.

Some may question why the group did not scout this rapid, opting instead to run on the experience and guidance of one member, even though his experience was extensive and his guidance correct. After this accident this site earned a reputation for needing scrupulous scouting and portage at low water. Stories of lost equipment and near misses do not seem to spread as far or penetrate as deeply as those involving personal injury or death.

Why, when there was an abundance of experienced, qualified, and professional rescuers at the scene, did the efforts fail? The boat, a Perception Dancer, showed hull deformity and creases, but the amount of boat deformity in itself should not have restricted exit. Water pressure on the deck probably kept Joe in his boat. Some controversy still exists as to the position of the kayak. A minority contend that the stern and not the bow was exposed and pointing to river right. In either case, whether the water was pushing him onto the back deck or tucked forward toward the front, the water pressure prohibited much movement. If the bow were exposed it would more easily explain a breathable air pocket, forcing Joe into a tucked forward position with water breaking over the back of his head. If the stern were exposed, some twisting would have been necessary to find the air pocket, which might explain a less stable position capable of deteriorating. Even though movement was evident for ten to twelve minutes, the degree of initial stability is questionable.

Still, a question has been raised concerning the possibility of the rope's being thrown to Joe having a destabilizing influence. This is possible, but the person belaying that rope was a professional river guide with years of experience, and he had witnessed the futile efforts made to reach the pinned boat. Three separate times the rope was laid in Joe's hand. If destabilizing was caused by the rope, perhaps it would have happened with the first throw. Perhaps not, but how many boaters would have stood by and not thrown a rope in the same situation?

Except for the presence of commercial rafts, the rescue might have taken hours. Tag or snag lining a wide river like the New is impractical. A kayaker made the eddy below the drop, but the paddler could not reach the pinned boat. Someone might have eventually gotten lucky with a heroic swim, but those who tried were unsuccessful. In general, the rescue was as efficient as could be expected. Considering these attempts, the best we can do is educate. The paddling community should know of the hidden danger of this particular spot at any negative gauge reading, but there is a general lesson to be learned from this account that is not restricted to a single geographic location: rivers change.

A boater must face these changes along with the more constant risks of whitewater, be he an intermediate eastern river runner like Joe Fleming or one of the best of western boaters, like Bob Porter, who died in California on Sunday, August 10, 1986, on the Kings River, near Kings Canyon National Park. The following account, only slightly edited, concludes this section. It comes from John Holland, who was paddling with Bob that final day.

Bob Porter

"This is my personal account of what happened based on what I saw and on talking to others who were present.

"The Garlic Falls run on the Kings is one of the most beautiful river canyons I have ever run. No doubt the Grand Canyon is bigger, Hells Canyon more famous, and Giant Gap narrower. But the granite walls, waterfalls plunging straight into the river, and views of distant mountains make it one of my favorites. Bob felt the same way.

"The accident site, in Rough Creek Rapid, is a place one does not normally go. The route is to the right side of a large rock at the beginning of the hardest rapid on the run. I had scouted the left side as a possible route, but it looked like I would pin or hit rocks at the bottom of this six- to eight-foot drop.

"A rock just under the surface pushed Bob off his line, over to the left side of the rock. He washed sideways against the boulder and began attempting to work his way back upstream so he could run to the right side of the boulder backwards. I believe he could have done this safely, but I am positive that he decided that he did not want to do it because he would not have been able to see where he was going at the top of a significant rapid. Instead, he chose to run forwards down the left.

"When Bob ran the left side, his bow pinned. He was stuck in a vertical position. Ted quickly threw a rope for Bob to hold on to, but he did not grab the rope. A second rope was thrown, and Bob managed to grab onto this one. Steve and Ted pulled Bob from his boat and into the water.

"Once in the water, Bob either deliberately let go of the rope or was so tired that he could not hold on. While swimming, Bob went under the surface between a large boulder and a smaller rock and disappeared completely. I never would have expected that a swimmer would have been pulled under there or that an underwater passage existed in that particular spot. Chuck Stanley agrees.

"Chuck made another trip down the Garlic Falls section on August 24. The water had dropped considerably, and he could see, but not recover, Bob's body. It was trapped in a passage between two rocks. His life jacket was on, and his feet were upstream. His boat was still jammed vertically on the left side of the boulder."

The body was recovered weeks later; rescuers reported that the situation was in fact a foot entrapment. There was no entanglement with the ropes, as the group had feared. Although this fact may have allayed the concerns of the rescuers, it is ironic that, in one of the few reported cases where rescuers were able to pull the victim free from a vertical entrapment using thrown ropes, he drowned in the ensuing swim.

One is tempted to invoke fate as an explanation, but the fact is that running class V rapids demands precise and reliable skills. The penalty for error is severe, even more so than on easier rapids. All river runners, not just those who attempt water of this difficulty, must never forget that accidents like these are one mistake away. Bob Porter was one of the best.

6

A reader may be forgiven if by this time he or she has reached a sort of gloomy impasse. So far in these accounts, boaters of different skill levels, from novice to expert, have died. Solo boaters and boaters in teams of the sport's greatest have died. Paddlers in novice groups and those surrounded by skilled and organized rescuers have died. It seems that anyone on whitewater can die there.

Anyone can. Some of us will, most of us won't. However, many of us will have a near miss or two. The reason is simple: people who spend time on rivers constantly face risk; injury and death are often only feet away or moments ahead, if we don't take proper actions. How many rivers, including our favorite and most familiar ones, are free of places we need to avoid and levels when we should not run them? Few, if any. But skill and experience, judgment and luck, training and good paddling partners—all these combine, most of the time, to keep us not out of danger, for danger is an integral part of our sport, but out of trouble.

How many times have all boaters made that crucial move to miss the pin, or broach, or surf, or swim? How many times have we failed to make the move but somehow gotten away with it? How many times have we not even known how close we came to disaster? to that lost throw rope, coiling snares in the current? to that unknown undercut, mouth open upstream, filtering the river through logs like a whale feeding? to that hidden piece of rebar, angled, waiting? to that pile of boulders with the unknown crevice, just large enough for a person to enter? These close calls are not documented.

In fact, only about half as many near misses as fatal accidents are reported in the River Safety Task Force Reports. Of the ones that are, many are simple tales focusing on injuries, injuries that often are an unavoidable part of the sometimes rough world of river running. But some are more than this; some are accounts of rescue, either self-rescue or rescue assisted by others, that may educate the boating community. They may also stand in optimistic contrast to the accounts of fatalities that make up the bulk of this book, where, in many cases, both victims and their would-be rescuers did everything they could and were unrewarded, unless a clear conscience can be considered a reward. In the following accounts, the people live.

Some of these near misses may be viewed as companion pieces to certain of the preceding accounts of fatalities. The parallels are often chilling. While it is sometimes impossible to compare rescue efforts point by point, because factors such as differences in the specifics of the situations or in the number of rescuers or the skill level, sometimes general comparisons may be possible simply because of the type of accident or even the nature of the account. Sometimes, however, there are no real comparisons at all.

Since these accounts report near misses, there is always a survivor, and often the survivor tells the tale. This point of view is quite unlike those of fatal accounts. For example, a pinned boater may be able to see rescuers with amazing clarity even though hidden from their view by sheets of water. Those who survive speak for those who don't, as if from beyond the watery grave. In the following accounts we must not imagine being the rescuer, but being the one who hopes for rescue. Generally, these records are so detailed that little analysis is needed. As always, in first-person accounts, we have retained the words of the original as much as possible, only making slight changes for clarity's sake.

This first account, by Jim Brooks Smith, tells of his pin and rescue on the Piney River in central Tennessee.

Jim Brooks Smith

"Our group put in on February 2, 1991. The Piney is a steep, technical run falling off the Cumberland Plateau south of Knoxville. Air temperature was to get into the 50's; water temperature was about the same.

"I was following the group when I came upon the rapid. I chose a slot to the left of a rock just left of center. I was not paddling hard enough to launch the boat, and I was not leaning back while going through the slot. I felt the bow catch; then the stern immediately dropped into a slot just past the lip of the drop. The water was flowing over my back and head; my boat was at a steep angle and well pinned.

My first move was to wiggle my boat with my hips, but there was no change. Breathing was okay, but the water was flowing across my face. I tried to stand straighter on my footpegs, but the water coming down on me made me feel as if I were being driven against the boat harder. Breathing was much more difficult in this position, causing me to swallow more water. I was surprised, scared, and wondering what would work to get me out of the boat. I began testing weight on one foot and trying to lift one knee above the rim of the cockpit.

"About that time Victor and Andy were on the left bank, and Jim Conerly had made it to the right. They quickly got a rope across and in front of my life jacket, against my chest. Shortly afterwards, the other Jim got to the right bank, and they got the rope secured. Looking to my left I could see Victor and Andy. They looked confident, and that reassured me. I could not turn to the right because the water was immersing me more that way. I yelled to Victor and Andy, 'What can I do next?' but they couldn't hear me. I knew they had done all they could to give me the opportunity to help myself. By pushing off my toes and leaning onto the rope, I could lift my left knee a little. The rope against my shorty life jacket constricted my breathing. I had thrown my paddle away because I needed both hands to push against the cockpit. The boat felt rigid and was not turning at all, despite my twisting movements. I swallowed more water doing this, and I cupped my hands over my mouth to keep water out.

"I think after a few unsuccessful tries, I began to quit, and panic. I remembered walks with my wife and wanting to see my daughter in the science fair. I think I teared up a little bit even with all the water rushing over my face.

After a few seconds, I returned with renewed efforts, determined to free myself. Somehow, I got my left knee above the rim of the cockpit. I could hear a cheer from everybody. That helped. Again I tried, slightly twisting to the right, and I got my left knee up on the cockpit rim. Quickly I pushed upright, bringing my right leg up. I had to get out of there, or I knew muscle cramps would occur. I wanted to go faster and just wrench myself over the side, but I was unsure of my balance. I had been in the water a while; my hands were numb, and I had swallowed as much water as air. Finally, I was crouched on the cockpit rim with my feet under me. Someone threw me a line, and the line on my chest was loosened. I looked, wrapped the new line under my elbow, and jumped. The water was frothy but shallow where I landed. I just held on as Jim pulled me into the eddy. He got me on a rock with my head lower than my feet, and I immediately belched out water.

"The other Jim, Victor, and Andy were looking for my boat, which had disappeared. At that moment I knew I would be okay, but I wondered how I would get out of there and what it would mean to all of us. They tried moving a throw rope over the place where my boat was. Later, Andy told me they could see my boat under the water.

"Andy found a large flat rock with which he and Victor weighted the throw rope and sunk it above the boat. After throwing the ropes across the river to loop the boat and pulling on them, they freed my kayak. Andy caught the boat, which had its stern bent up toward the sky. He jumped up and down on the boat, which straightened it some, and ferried it across the river to me. Victor hung it between two rocks, and we sat on the boat's bottom. This straightened it enough to paddle. My spray skirt had washed off along with an air bag, throw rope, water bottle, and paddle. Jim had a breakdown paddle, and Andy found my spray skirt. We estimated that I had been in the water twelve to fifteen minutes, and we had used another hour getting the boat out, so it was about 2:00 P.M. We got moving.

"My paddle and throw rope were around the next bend. I was very apprehensive and paddled conservatively the rest of the way to the take-out. However, I had a heightened sense of the beauty of this river gorge. We took out about 5:30 P.M.

"In retrospect, I thought of other things I might have done. I had been clumsy starting out; I should have paddled hard and leaned back going over the ledge. I might have used my paddle as a pole to help pry myself out of the boat. My throw bag should have been tied in more securely and near my grasp; then I could have used a carabiner and hooked it to the broach loop in the front of my cockpit. At one point near the end of the ordeal, I thought I had swallowed too much water and I was weakening. I'd read it was better to use all your strength for one great attempt to free yourself. I guess that's a judgment call.

"That morning I had taped a weak ankle and decided to leave my breakdown paddle in Chattanooga. I had driven hundreds of miles and had had four hours sleep. At my age, I cannot rebound as quickly as I used to. I let too many details slide by. I am glad I have the opportunity to paddle another day.

"The other paddlers acted immediately and stabilized me. There was no wasted energy or confusion in their efforts to rescue me. They were poised and encouraging. If you get in the wrong place at the wrong time, you had better be with the right people. I am thankful I was with some competent, well-trained paddlers to whom I owe a debt of gratitude. I hope this report will help warn and instruct others in some way."

Others must have thought the same things Jim thought, others who were vertically pinned listening for encouragement from their would-be rescuers, feeling ropes come and go, trying to understand the hurried rescue efforts from their own constrained points of view. Others must have felt the same emotional juxtapositions—combinations of acceptance and defiance, of regret for things forever undone and of drive to live and do them, of panic and disbelief. Darkness followed for many, or light, or whatever comes after, but not for Jim. And not for Cris Leonard, who tells in the next account of his lengthy pin at Sweet's Falls on the Gauley—in an open canoe.

Cris Leonard

"On the second day of the Coastal Canoeists' Labor Day weekend trip in 1978, September 3rd, a group of twenty-one boats put in on the Gauley River immediately below Summersville Lake. It was 9:30 A.M., and a dam release was in progress. The Corps of Engineers was discharging slightly more than 1000 cfs. As trip leader, this was the water I wanted.

"Sweet's Falls drops ten feet. Most of the water flows right over the middle of this drop. It flows down and into a very swift moving pool below the Falls. There is very little backwash here, no keeper, but the pool is too deep and the current much too swift to stand in. This is where my trip ended in near disaster.

"Don Bowman and Jim Magurno both swamped at the foot of this rapid. I made the third attempt. I'm not sure but that over-confidence was not a factor. The rescue lines were out, there were boats and the water below me, there were twenty good men on the water, and I was having a great day.

"My entry into Sweet's Falls was too far to the left. Drawing right, I lost forward momentum. The bow of my canoe dropped into the pool below, hit the riverbed with the impact of a sledgehammer, and stuck fast. I pitched forward hard. Somehow I got my right leg over the thwart in front of me. That thwart caught me in the crotch as my left leg slid under it. The Gauley River was now breaking over my back and head, pinning me to the thwart. To complicate things further, my boat collapsed partially under the force of the water—enough to assure that the thwart had a viselike grip across my left thigh. I was trapped and I was scared.

"Old Man River was doing his best to force my head into the water, gathering in my boat and further folding it into the river below me. I gripped a thwart in front of me to hold my head and upper torso erect—and the water continued to pound away at me. After screaming and whistle blowing, I realized that the group was aware of my predicament, and I settled down to await help. Sure enough, a rescue line entered the current and reached me. They had stretched a line across the river and lowered it to me, hoping I could get my arm over it and that they could thereby pull me from the boat. Not a chance! My boat had to come out for me to come out. While hoping they could get the end of a rope to me to tie to my boat (no one else could possibly reach the boat to do it), I remembered that my own rescue bag was within reach. It was a lot of work to tie my rope to a thwart, and I realized that hypothermia was coming on rapidly. I threw the rope downstream and waited.

"Another half hour passed. Things didn't look too good. I was not in a state of panic or shock. I was going to die that afternoon. The cold water was beating me. It was just a matter of time. I was mentally and emotionally prepared to die but determined not to give up. There were twenty good men out there pulling for me. After a while, I slumped forward, propping my head up on one hand. I rested, hoping to conserve energy. Time passed. I got a second wind. I know I had been motionless for a long time and thought, 'Those guys think that I am dead!' I sat erect, reached as high as I could, and felt my hand break the water. I later learned that this signal was extremely encouraging to my friends.

"The number of rescuers had increased now by two more groups of paddlers arriving at Sweet's Falls. Between rest periods I raised my left hand two more times.

"The Corps of Engineers had cut the release from Summersville Lake by 300 cfs at 1:00 P.M., so perhaps the water had dropped a little. Maybe the boat had shifted a little. Several men were now pulling the rescue rope from river right; perhaps the group had moved it slightly. No good! They were ready to have a line ferried to river left when Randy Perkins noticed that something had changed. He ran to the water's edge, waving and exhorting, 'Pull!' And pull they did. My boat rolled free. This brought me around in a real hurry. I was able to kick and wiggle loose. My life jacket kept me afloat, and when the group saw that I could hold my head up, twenty men cried.

"Two kayakers reached me in seconds. I didn't know them, but I'd never been happier to see anyone. They towed me into six inches of water, but I couldn't stand or walk; I was carried out of the river.

"One of the late arrivals, Carl Lundgren, took charge of hypothermia treatment and bandaging and splinting. We were all thankful for his presence; his knowledge of emergency first aid was most helpful. A litter was improvised from my canoe, and nine men carried me down the railroad tracks that led out of the gorge. Soon two troopers, called earlier, showed up on dirt bikes. One left to report our location, and eventually a railroad company vehicle picked us up and drove us to the Peters Creek take-out, where the ambulance was waiting. We reached the Summersville Hospital at midnight, ten hours after the ordeal had begun.

"I'm a very fortunate young man. I suffered only muscle and tissue damage to both legs, several stitches in my right ankle, and time on crutches. I could be dead. The lessons that we learned that day are numerous. Without Carl Lundgren, I would have suffered more. The emergency first aid training and experience of the other participants on that trip was very limited. My group tried everything possible, within and beyond reason, to get me out of there, yet some of us feel that the rescue operation needed a leader. I wasn't well prepared. Had someone else been trapped, and had I needed to go for help or to notify the authorities, other than the Peters Creek take-out I didn't know a way out of that gorge. My personal attitudes towards river paddling have changed.

"I'll probably paddle the Gauley River again. But on all rivers, I'll look at each rapid with a 'What if something goes wrong?' or 'What can go wrong?' attitude, as opposed to the 'I stand a real good chance' or 'He ran (or swam) it; I can do that well' or 'There are good safety and rescue personnel out here today' or 'I've been having such a good day' point of view."

Cris ends his story in a reflective tone, telling us what the experience taught him—that his attitude had been cavalier, that he should take the pin as a lesson. He is grateful for the chance to learn, knowing that many in his position were not given one. How often in the years that followed his pin did he think about it? How many times while driving to work, for instance, did his mind wander to the world of what-ifs? What if his throw bag had not been in reach? What if he had not been able to breathe quite as well? What if there were not enough people to pull his boat free? How long would he have lasted? What else could he have done? Would he ever have been saved at all?

The next boater also was given a lesson, a chance to wonder, an opportunity to ask questions that might have caused him to reflect on his whitewater attitude, the chances he took, the reasons he took them. He probably did reflect; everyone would. But at the risk of being unfair to him, the circumstances surrounding his death on whitewater three years later make one ask if the lessons he learned were heartfelt.

On March 29, 1979, Chuck Rawlins was part of a trip led by Pete Skinner,

of the American Whitewater Association, in New York State. The trip consisted of two runs, the second on Kaaterskill Creek, which flows adjacent to
Route 23-A near Palenville. Chuck tells his own story.

Chuck Rawlins

"I paddled across the flat pool looking for the broken slot in the
first three-foot ledge that would define the line for the eight- to ten-
foot drop immediately following. It didn't reveal itself until the last
minute, but there it was, not even a correction stroke needed, nothing
ahead but a whoopee time. The slot is smooth, a little froth in the
platform before the longer whoopee ahead. The adrenaline is up some,
but a more straightforward run couldn't have been imagined.

"As I start to drop through the first slot, the boat begins to find
its own way, going with the flow, and then—damn it!—everything
stops. All the slack in my posture disappears instantly, the forward
momentum stops, and the bow is buried. Very quickly the water
flows up the back deck against my back and up over my head.

"Well, suddenly a simple run becomes somewhat more complicated. Still, no great concern, some wiggling and juggling will reveal
the direction to push, pull, or shove. Breathing is no problem. I'm in
an envelope and visibility straight ahead is good. In fact, there's Larry
Osgood on the right shore of the lower pool taking pictures, but why
did he drop his camera and run back beyond my right-side periph-
eral view?

"Now I begin to feel some concern. The boat won't budge, not
even a little bit. The only water I can reach is too aerated to be
effective; I can get some resistance but no real response. I had felt a
momentary sense of panic when the stern first sank and from some
minimal instability as the kayak settled against the bottom of the
slot. However, I now began to consider my options.

"The water was very cold, but I had been boating all day in full
wet suit and paddling gear. However, as this was going to be a very
quick run, I hadn't bothered to don pogies. When my hands were in
the water this was a problem, but if I pulled them into my chest they
could actually get relatively dry and warm up.

"The next thing I recall thinking about was just how stable I was.

Some paddle probing quickly reconfirmed that I was very stable. I then gave some thought to jumping out but quickly abandoned that option for the moment, as I would have had to give up the paddle to pull it off, and some tentative experimentation had convinced me that an all-out effort presented the real possibility of folding the boat around my lower legs before they cleared the cockpit.

"At this point I remember thinking that I had done about all I could do from my position, given that there were several very hip river people ashore and they were surely getting their act together. I was stable, relatively warm, and had no breathing problems. As far as I was concerned, I was in a good position for thirty to sixty minutes while things were getting organized on the shore. 'They must be very busy,' I thought. 'All the activity must be from my rear, upriver, as it were.'

"My main concern at this point was in keeping my hands warm and in being ready when real rescue efforts began. My feeling was of absolute confidence that things would resolve themselves.

"'Now what the hell is happening?' I thought. 'Something is changing and I haven't the faintest notion what it is. I can barely hang on to my paddle and I'm being tipped over. Maybe there's a river monster in here.'

"I retrieve my right blade from some very solid force on the right side. Now I'm having to fight off a bit of panic. The reason is that something has changed but I can't figure out what it is. I'm trying to figure out what's changed, very tentatively probing the right-side water, when again I'm nearly flipped. This time, however, I hear a voice say, 'Stop pulling.' It's Kevin Hanrahan, and he's worked his way out to a point where he can grab my paddle.

"At this point, things happen very suddenly. I want to cooperate with the rescue efforts, so I yell to Kevin to try again, but I don't pull too hard as I'm very concerned about an off-balance shift to my right. Our first joint effort immediately results in a complete flip. For the first time I have a feeling of—panic?—the word doesn't seem right—extreme concern?—not much better. I'm now upside down, head underwater, still in the slot, with tremendous pressure against my back and head. The rotation hadn't done a blessed thing toward freeing the boat from the slot, and I was having a tremendously difficult time with my wet exit.

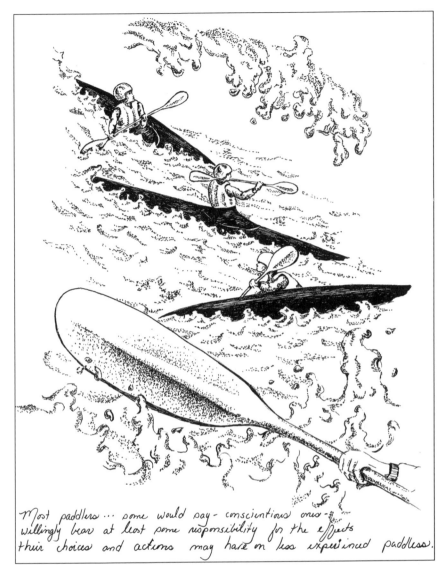

Most paddlers ... some would say - conscientious ones - willingly bear at least some responsibility for the effects their choices and actions may have on less experienced paddlers.

"I was hanging upside down in a very fast slot, with the force of heavy water pushing forward. I think it's at times like these that the psychology of survival begins to assert itself. There was no doubt in my mind that I would get out. At the risk of sounding vain and/or smug, I can actually recall considering just what it was going to take to get my legs out without breaking my knees by bending them in the opposite direction. Succeed I did, and as I popped up, there were Kevin and Peter.

"Kevin grabbed my arm and in turn grabbed Peter's arm, who was trying to hang on to a very cold, smooth, slippery ledge. They were both imploring me to swim.[1] The urge was there—oh, was it ever!—but why didn't the legs respond? I twice came to the brink of the lower drop and looked over, but I didn't like the prospects, as we were off to the right side of the main channel and some very nasty-looking splat-type rocks were immediately below us. On the other hand, we weren't making any progress towards getting upstream to the ledge under which Peter had found refuge. I yelled at Kevin to let me go so as to get me into the main channel with its clear drop into the pool below. The actual drop was uneventful.

"My knees were not broken but were very severely strained. Two weeks of prescribed bed rest coincided very neatly with the two week New York subway strike, and an additional six weeks of progressively less and less hobbling brought this event to a happy ending. In retrospect, I think I should have made a stronger effort to communicate with the shoreside rescue effort and informed them of my condition. This would have afforded the rescue effort much more time for a somewhat more sophisticated attempt."

Communication between victim and rescuers, when possible, is an advantage that should be used to its fullest potential. In the preceding account, Chuck Rawlins writes that he should have been clearer about his degree of stability, about his condition in general, allowing a more careful rescue to be planned. In the following record, Mike Malone tells of surviving a heads-up broach in a C-1. Communication was good during his rescue, at least until the end. Other than this criticism, which Mike makes himself, there is little to call wrong in this rescue and much to call right. Well-trained people worked carefully to effect a save. Mike does, however, point out the significant reason for getting into trouble in the first place.

---

[1]Chuck's absolute confidence that things would work out was rewarded because of the quick efforts, at considerable risk, of his paddling partners. However, this pin was not to be the last dire whitewater situation Chuck found himself in. In 1982 he drowned on the South Fork of the Clearwater. The account appears earlier in this book.

Mike Malone

"On the last Sunday in April 1983, Denis and George McLane and I decided to finish our paddling day with a quick run on the Chichester Creek, a tributary of the Esopus Creek at Phoenicia, New York. We had run the tight, steep (eighty feet per mile), rock-choked stream two weeks before on a sunny snowmelt day at about the same level, but this run was to take place during a rainstorm on a raw 50 degree day. We'd been unable to run the Chichester much since the fall of 1979, when a flood left a great deal of wood in the stream.

"We were paddling C-1s; mine was a new low-volume racing boat. I had torn one of the thigh-strap carriers out earlier in the day but was confident that I'd be able to roll if need be since my lower thighs were jammed solidly under the cockpit rim. The boat also was not air-bagged, but it was walled from bow to stern with ethafoam, the saddle having been formed from the wall. I was convinced that I was sufficiently well equipped to undertake this final run of the day.

"At one of the more exciting points along the Chichester, the creek makes a slight left-hand turn, bordered by a straight wall of shale on the river right. The first of two large holes forms on the left at this spot, leaving as the desired line the pillow extending along the right-hand wall. The second of the two holes occurs on river right about two boat lengths downstream and obstructs approximately two-thirds of the thirty-foot-wide stream. The trick to running this particular rapid is to bypass the first hole by maneuvering to the right along the wall, and then to cut left into the slower water after the hole in order to buy the necessary time to proceed hard left around the second hole. The next hundred yards downstream are narrow and fast, with the smooth wall continuing along the right.

"I was, perhaps, a bit lazy in making my left-hand move after the first hole and found myself back-endered into the second. After flushing out of the hole, I had to pull my knees into the boat to begin my roll. It worked, but my skirt had opened and I was running sideways, paddle-side downstream (luckily) and approaching a large flat rock that looked inviting at the time.

"As I hit the rock, I attempted to lurch myself up onto it, boat and all, with the intention of putting back in on the downstream side. Suddenly, the boat turned its cockpit downstream and slid down the face of the rock with my right foot still trapped inside. This left me precariously sandwiched between my boat and the rock, my knees against the deck and my right armpit leaning against the thin top edge of that once-inviting ledge. The boat was riding against my ribs and breathing was exceedingly difficult, so I pushed with my left arm, still thinking in terms of hauling everything up onto the rock. But the boat went down instead of up, easing my breathing but leaving me trapped.

"Flexing my muscles did nothing to dislodge the boat from my foot, but the situation was stable—both the McLanes are rescue-oriented, and I was heads-up pinned. I knew that there were steel pry bars in Denis's shop back in Phoenicia and that Bobbie and Drew Reynolds were sitting in their van up on Route 214, watching our run. Ropes were in the van, and I had confidence in the abilities of our rescue team.

"My hopes sank a little as I watched Denis get caught in the upper hole and then swim past me. Turning my upper body to my right permitted the river to hold me a bit more upright, but the cold water was beginning to take its toll. George was alert to my situation and eddied out after the first hole. He then swam to the eddy behind my rock by starting about fifty feet upstream of me. I described my position to him, and George verified it by feeling my ankle and boat with one hand. We both knew that I needed only an inch leeway to get free, but he could not move the boat with his legs. We discussed using a safety rope tied under my arms, but I only wanted such a precaution if the rescue was going to take a long time, since my position presented the possibility that the rope could become caught around the base of the rock should I become free of my boat. I suggested trying the steel bars back home, but we decided to try a nearby log first to save time.

"Drew, who had by then appeared on the scene, overthrew George when he tossed the log, but Denis was now approaching the eddy behind the rock and was able to retrieve the makeshift tool. The log worked on the second attempt, although the maneuver I made to free myself scared my rescuers because they thought I had completely lost it. I felt my foot come free and, fearing that the boat might break, untwisted my body to get out. This put me entirely underwater, but I swam out cleanly. Later, on shore, the heater in the van helped my early stage of hypothermia, and after about fifteen minutes I finally stopped shivering. The total amount of time that had elapsed with me in the water had probably been no more than ten minutes.

"The aftermath of this incident involved the recovery of my boat on Wednesday. By that time it had folded, but it was repairable. An examination of the rock at lower water revealed a flat platform perched upon a number of smaller rocks. A tree stump also wedged under it had saved my life.

"The single most contributory factor to my mishap was lack of proper outfitting. A C-1 cannot possibly be rolled if you can't stay in it. My failure to read and identify a badly undercut rock compounded my error, although all I could have done was bail out earlier. A safety rope secured under my arms might have been prudent if it could have extended from the right-hand bank, but from where my land-based rescuers were operating, a rope might have snagged under the rock when I attempted to swim free.

"Communication between victim and rescuers is vital and was good in this situation; however, I should have informed George what I was doing before going underwater to free myself. I was thankful that we had all participated in rescue clinics and that I had gathered some experience, voluntarily clearing streams and rescuing pinned equipment in the past. All of these exercises made us more aware of the river's forces and the possibilities available with the items we had at hand."

Training, experience, communication, teamwork—these, in addition to good luck in the form of a tree stump that kept his C-1 from sinking deeper, were enough to let Mike and his friends succeed. In the equation of river rescue—Judgment + Training + Equipment + Luck = Result—only the first three factors can be controlled. Luck, or, for those who do not believe in luck, the pivotal specifics of a given circumstance, cannot be controlled. We cannot entirely escape the dangers of whitewater, and one may wonder if the sport would hold nearly the same appeal if we could, but we owe it to ourselves and to our fellow boaters—and perhaps to the river itself—to fight the good fight. Anything less shows a lack of respect. Think carefully, learn and practice skills, have rescue gear available. Mike and his friends followed this advice on their afternoon recreational run. The professional racers in the following account did, too. One who broached on a tree is especially glad they did.

Kathy Bolyn

On July 2, 1990, Kathy Bolyn, a nationally known racer, river runner, and instructor, was training with a group of elite wildwater racers on the Savage River, a premier whitewater racing river near Bloomington, Maryland. The water, released from the bottom of a lake, is extremely cold, so time is of the essence when making rescues here. Because of the stream's small size and intermittent flow, downed trees have always been a concern for race organizers. Although the tree that caused this accident was spotted and trimmed by organizers the day before the event, the water was low then, and the tree was not cut back far enough, leaving Memorial Rock Rapid extremely hazardous for racers training the next day.

On their first run, Kathy Bolyn and the group missed the tree. The danger frightened them, but the group felt they were "here to do a job" and decided to continue practicing. However, they also elected to travel as a close-knit group, and several boaters picked up lightweight rescue gear. On the second run, the first part of the group came through the drop fine. Kathy, leading the second wave, broached on the tree as she tried to turn in the drop. She was able to duck under the eighteen-inch trunk, but her boat, equipped with both vertical and lateral walls, was pushed against a five-inch-diameter limb sticking down into the river. The kayak quickly wrapped, crushing Kathy's legs together so that she could not exit. She was left with her body facing upstream, holding on to the same branch that held her boat.

The group reacted immediately to her predicament. Jeff Huey and Paul Grabow climbed onto the tree trunk and approached Kathy from river right. As they got close, the tree sagged, deterring them from advancing farther. On river left, others in the group threw Kathy a rope. By tying this to a nearby branch, she was able to lean back against it and gain support, stabilizing her position for the time being.

Although well dressed in a shorty wet suit and dry top, which kept her from suffering too much from the cold, Kathy was in considerable pain. Her position was stable, but she was completely helpless. She kept calm by concentrating on what still felt good and on the beauty of the surrounding river. Her greatest fear was that she might pass out.

Since the group was unable to help further with the tools they had, Mary Hipsher approached a local landowner for the loan of a saw. When she returned, the saw was ferried to Paul Grabow, who began to work first on the bow of Kathy's boat and then on the tree limb that pinned her. As Paul did this, Jeff Huey passed a second rope to Kathy from river right. She untied the first rope so that when the limb gave way she could grab the second and swim to safety. The plan worked.

On the river-right bank she was eased into a kayak; she made the ferry across the fast, choppy river to the left shore. There, a waiting ambulance transferred her to a helicopter for a flight to a hospital in Cumberland, Maryland. She was discovered to have torn ligaments in her right knee, as well as minor crush wounds on both legs. She faced an extended recovery time of more than a year.

Memorial Rock Rapid does have a rocky left-hand sneak route. It has been used in the past and was runnable the day of the accident for those uncomfortable with the tree's dangers. However, as whitewater racing has become increasingly competitive, pressures on the top racers to perform have increased. Some of these competitive pressures undoubtedly contributed to Kathy's broach. But the fundamental component of whitewater competition is still whitewater, with all the normal choices and risks.

Some racers felt that the course should have been thoroughly checked and patrolled before the practice runs. The tree was clearly in the way; those who had cut it back earlier apparently did not realize just how far the water was going to rise. Still, competitors must assume the responsibility for assessing these dangers; there is no way a championship-level course can be made risk free. Since safety personnel cannot cover the entire wildwater course as in a slalom, racers must be prepared to rescue themselves and to assist others. They must also be prepared to back off when they encounter conditions they consider unsafe, reporting the problem to the race organizer.

The rescue itself was a textbook example of effective organization and execution. The group reacted quickly, stabilizing the victim and extracting her from the pin. All members should be commended for their teamwork, ingenuity, and courage. They should also be commended for their wise decision to make their practice runs together.

The preceding account points out the usefulness of a saw in many pinning situations. While it is probably unrealistic to expect wildwater racers to carry rescue gear beyond the essentials, it is not at all unrealistic to hope that private boaters will carry more than a throw bag and a couple of carabiners. Boating is fun. But all boaters, and especially those who mostly make short trips on very well known, popular play rivers, sometimes forget that every day is not destined to end smoothly with tying the boats on the car and driving back into town. We are not designed by nature for running rivers, no matter how much we might feel at home on the water. We need tools just to be there; during a rescue we need the right tools for a chance to come back.

Imagine the following situation: you're dropped off with a companion or two in the middle of a beautiful but remote forest. The weather is bad, so without the right clothes you're likely to be wet and cold for hours. You know the way out, but you also know that the path you must follow is rugged and sometimes treacherous. Many obstacles stand between you and your journey's end—cliffs, blowdowns, darkness if you take too long. Many hidden dangers await—unknown holes to break a leg in, dead trees ready to fall if you bump against them. Despite the dangers, or perhaps because of them, the trip excites you. You're confident; you have trusted companions; you have the proper gear. What items do you take for comfort and safety?

What did you take with you on your last boating trip?

In the following account a knife is needed. The victim has one, but his condition won't let him use it. Since the river is popular, help arrives in time.

John Norton

On October 23, 1982, John Norton and a friend were finishing a run on the Ocoee River, near Benton, Tennessee. The Ocoee, from dam #2 to the powerhouse below, is one of the most popular class III+-IV runs in the East and is used by many thousands of people each year without incident. John's trip was routine until the last rapid, when his partner spilled. As John ferried after his friend's boat near Hell Hole, he realized too late how close he was to the bridge pier just below. As he made contact, his boat flipped upstream and was solidly pinned. He bailed out, but one of his feet became tangled in his thigh straps. The current pushed him under, and although he could struggl. up for an occasional breath, he was losing strength quickly.

On the shore, a group of professional guides from High Country in Atlanta were setting up a throw line for an oncoming trip. They saw the pin but did not realize for several minutes that John was still trapped in his boat. Once they realized what was going on, they leapt into action, running to the bridge[2] and lowering a guide to the pinned boat nearly twenty feet below. The guide, Karen Berry, found secure footing on top of the pinned canoe. She tied a line to John, allowing his head to be pulled above the water. Realizing that John was tangled, she called for a knife to be lowered and cut him free. After this, Karen tied John into a Swiss seat and the guides above pulled him up to safety. John was evacuated by ambulance to a local hospital, where he was treated and released.

It should be noted that John had a knife, but the force of the current kept him from using it. His only mistake was being in a bad place, a not uncommon situation during rescues, which calls for extra care during these times. John's rescue, swift and well organized, is characteristic of professional guides who have responded many times over the years to accidents on private trips. This is one positive side effect of raft pollution.

Although the presence of professional rescuers does not guarantee success, it certainly improves the chances. Many people on the river (and off) owe their lives to the skilled efforts of professionals who happen to be on the scene. It is difficult to imagine a better illustration of this truth than the following account, the first of four very different near misses that all involve swims.

Near Miss on the James River

In the summer of 1986 a group of professional guides and river-rescue instructors were boating for pleasure on the James River in Virginia when a pair of tubers attempted to run Hollywood Rapid

---

[2]This bridge has been replaced by one that is supported only on the banks, removing the danger of similar pins that were common at this site.

(class IV), the biggest drop on the river. The tubers were not wearing life jackets when they were pulled out of their tubes in the top hole; one swam to safety while the other, a woman, was swept downstream. Nancy Roberts White, of the Wilderness Challenge School in Chesapeake, Virginia, describes the rescue.

"I watched the woman wash through the second hydraulic. I shouted at her not to stand up. When she disappeared, my stomach turned. With three whistle blasts I signaled Glen Carlson, pointing to where I had seen her last. I shouted, 'She's still underwater!' His face registered dismay as he paddled, straining to find her in the churning water. I knew she had probably caught her foot on something because she looked as if she was trying to stand up to get a breath of air.

"Seconds seemed like hours as I scanned the water; then I heard Mike's whistle blasts by a boulder ten yards away. They had found her! The first priority was to get her head above water. Maneuvering behind the boulder, Glen and Mike scrambled out of their boats and grabbed throw lines. The woman was underwater and could not be helped by a kayak until brought to the surface. I was sitting on a midstream boulder opposite Glen, who threw me a line to anchor with a sitting hip belay.

"I knew a stabilization line, or tag line—a rope strung horizontally in front of the victim—was our goal. If she was conscious, she might be able to grab the line and gain enough stability to lift her head up. If not, we would convert our rope to a snag line by weighting it and lowering it under the water, then pulling it upstream to dislodge the victim. Mike remained in his kayak in case she came free.

"Both techniques sound simple but are difficult to carry out. We maneuvered the line upstream and attempted to hook it under the victim. The pressure on the rope from the force of the current was unbelievable. I tightened my grasp and pulled harder upstream. Suddenly I heard Glen shout, 'She's conscious! She's got the rope!' She struggled to the surface and instantly was freed from whatever had trapped her. She was floating downstream. Glen and Mike, both in boats now, raced to recover our semiconscious victim. Quickly turning her faceup, and paddling carefully, they were able to position her between their kayaks and maneuver her into the eddy behind my rock.

"As we pulled her onto the rock I quickly assessed her condition: semiconscious, hypothermic, but definitely breathing. A deformed and discolored foot and ankle and a protruding bone indicated at least a compound fracture. Much to my relief, our victim-turned-patient began to gasp, sputter, and cough and began sobbing with relief as we wrapped her in polypropylene jackets. We treated her for shock. A park ranger arrived and shouted that a rescue squad was on its way. Total elapsed time was under ten minutes."

This was one lucky person. It's not every time that you screw up on the river in front of a group of river guide/rescue trainer/EMTs. This is a good argument for all boaters to learn the rescue and first aid skills that made the difference on the James. The stabilization line used here is fundamental to many rescue efforts, especially on narrow rivers.

In the following report, told by the survivor, Steve Groetzinger, rescue does not come courtesy of a group of whitewater professionals. Rather, one skilled boater is able to help the victim from his pinned kayak. After this, however, things turn chaotic.

Steve Groetzinger

"No sooner had I become comfortable on the Gauley River than in 1982 I had the unsettling experience of helping to carry out the body of a kayaker who drowned in Initiation Rapid, the first major drop on the river. (Bob O'Connor's accident is reported in the previous chapter.) He had eddied out on river right just above the main drop, which unfortunately feeds into a sluice that empties into a toilet bowl suckhole and disappears under a very large rock. This experience left me with put-in jitters for several seasons thereafter.

"It was a warm, sunny October morning in fall 1989, and I was feeling very laid back as I climbed into my kayak and shoved out into the Gauley River. Many of my paddling friends were there, and Cindy, my wife of less than four months, was riding in a raft with several other friends on an accompanying commercial trip. The rafts headed downstream as we hardboaters played and acclimated ourselves to this wonderful river.

As we approached Initiation, I was as comfortable as a human can be, chitchatting with Bob Miller as we reached the top drop of the rapid. In an instant, my calm demeanor was totally destroyed when I realized I was in the far right eddy above Initiation.

"My first thought was 'How did I get here?' This is an absolutely horrible place to be, and any idiot knows not to go near the right side! The fatal accident that happened here flashed through my mind. The boater and his boat were sucked vertically into the hole and under the rock, disappearing for the rest of the day. I figured the only thing I could do was to paddle hard and hope that I could bounce over that death-trap hole.

"I realized that this strategy was a semifailure as the front of my kayak slammed into the rock and pinned. The tremendous amount of water pouring over my back and neck created a three-foot rooster-tail. My boat was slightly bent, and the extreme water pressure was pushing me down into the boat, making it difficult for me to peel myself out of the cockpit. Nevertheless, it was easy to remain calm. I could breathe with no trouble, and the water was particularly warm. So long as I made no sudden movements, my boat was not going to slip into that dreaded hole, and my friends were going to get a rope to me.

"The rescue was not a simple task. Initiation is a steep drop with lots of weird currents at the bottom. There was only one skinny rock from which to throw a rope. Alex Hardy was amazing. He somehow paddled through a whirlpool, slithered up this steep rock, and managed to throw a rope right to me. I gingerly pulled myself out of the boat, being cautious not to fall. This is where my luck really turned bad. The rock was unbelievably slippery, and my feet came out from under me. I immediately fell into that hole that I was so worried about. I knew this was getting to be serious! At this instant, my brain went into that 'supercomputer' mode that you hear about when people get into dangerous situations. In hindsight, this was the amazing thing about this horrifying experience. Somehow, as if someone programmed a portion of my brain to take control, every single synapse was energized with one goal in mind: survival.

"At this point, I was several feet underwater and could not breathe. The water was pushing down on my head with the force of a hurricane. Fortunately, though, I still had the rope. I began to try to climb out of the hole in the rock, but the force of the water was impossible to combat. I could not move.

"I stopped to think, holding my breath. How could this happen? Did I not realize how important it was for me to get out of this thing? Remember what happened to the other guy a few years ago? I thought, 'You just have to try harder, Steve.' I really tried with all my might this time, but my efforts were absolutely fruitless.

"It was time to stop and think. If I panicked at this moment, it would be all over. Strength was not going to get me out of this predicament alive, and I had to spend whatever time I had left thinking up a strategy. Something dawned on me. Maybe this is one of those dreams where, at the last instant, I take a gasp and wake up. It sure seemed real, but just in case, I tried to suck in a minute amount of water just to test this hypothesis.

"The dream theory was wrong. This was the real thing. Suppose I just wait for the other guys to get to the rock where Alex was holding the rope? With enough of them up there, surely they could pull me out of this. I began to wonder what they were doing up there and could only picture the pandemonium. But there was no way that they were going to get through that whirlpool and onto that little rock in time to pull me up alive. What was I going to do?

"I grew despondent. I began to feel sorry for myself and wondered how painful this was going to be. What were my friends thinking up there? What was Cindy going to say when she heard? How would she take it, and what kind of a fix am I leaving her in? What a jerk I must be. I threw away a pretty good life doing something stupid. Kayaking was great, but it wasn't worth this.

"All these thoughts probably happened over a span of thirty seconds, the longest thirty seconds I have ever known. Then a critical new idea came to me. Where does all this water go? It must come out somewhere! Why not just let go of this rope? Suppose the hole is smaller than I am? I'd be finished for certain. Then again, if I just hang on to this rope, I will eventually pass out, and I would rather try to squeeze through a hole in the rock when I am conscious.

"It became clear that this was my only choice. I would curl into a ball and let go of the rope. If I felt myself hitting rocks, I would try different positions, and maybe one of them would produce the optimum shape to slip through this theoretical lifesaving hole.

"I let go of the rope. Meanwhile, topside, Alex felt the rope sud-denly slacken. Since he was pulling with all his might, he fell back-wards off the rock. My friends told me afterwards that he turned white as a sheet, thinking that the rescue attempt had come to a tragic conclusion.

"In an instant, I saw daylight. I flushed under the rock like a supersonic jet, and this was the most beautiful sunlight I had ever seen. Unfortunately, this scene was not quite over. Upon exiting from the rock, I got caught in a hydraulic and went for a long series of somersaults. In spite of this, I had a smile on my face. All I had to do was dive down, and I'd be out of this thing. It worked, and I was able to savor the tastiest breath of air I have ever known! The ordeal was over.

"I thought, 'I guess kayaking is worth it after all.' I still enjoy the Gauley, but I'll never get to the right side of Initiation again."

Despite the light tone at the end of his tale, which is understandable since he had just made it, both cold calculation and luck played a part in Steve's survival. It is possible that taking time at the beginning of the rescue to gather personnel would have allowed for a more controlled effort, a point made in reference to the attempted rescue of Bob O'Connor. But the difficulties of getting to this site and the great danger faced by rescuers of falling into the hole there are also made clear. Over the years, several boaters have flushed through this dangerous passage and one more has drowned. Since debris may block openings, committing to a no-return swim is a perilous option. Once caught in the hole, however, unable to climb out, did Steve really have any other options?

In the next report, five boaters have a close call where the only good option would have been to avoid the problem entirely. Fred Seifer, the boater who tells the story, wholeheartedly agrees.

Fred Seifer

"Dave Jordan and Bruce Hayes had dropped in on Monday evening, July 3, 1989, after spending four days paddling in West Virginia. I had not planned on paddling on July 4th, but I was juiced up with the arrival of Dave and Bruce. On our way to the Watauga in North

Carolina, we checked the Doe Gorge, which proved to be too low to run, estimating the level at 300 cfs. When we crossed the Elk River, we knew the Watauga would be cooking, as the Elk was screaming out of its banks. The bridge at the put-in for the Watauga was completely submerged. The river was into the trees—flood-stage Watauga!

"Obviously, the Watauga Gorge was out of the question. Leon then suggested running the upper section, above the gorge, stating that it would be a 'quick flush.' I wasn't too excited about a 'quick flush,' as it didn't seem much like a challenge. I did, however, decide that I might as well paddle, as I had driven all that way and wanted to wet my boat. The water was typical flood stage—fast, scurrile, and muddy brown.

"We all hit the river with hopeful anticipation. Bruce took the lead, with Dave and me approximately thirty yards behind and Leon and R. B. bringing up the rear. I kept a watchful eye upstream, spying for floating trees and other flotsam. After approximately five minutes on the river, things started getting interesting—big scurrile water, eight- to ten-foot waves, and pushy crosscurrents. I thought to myself, 'This is no flush.' Then we encountered two big holes, back to back, that we all managed to maneuver through safely. The adrenaline was pumping and the anxiety level was up.

"At this point, I knew that this was in fact no flush, but rather a locomotive out of control, a train I no longer wished to be riding. Unfortunately, there was no way off. The water was moving at approximately ten to twenty miles per hour (it seemed like a hundred), and before I could eddy out—where were the eddies?—I saw Bruce Hayes drop into the ugliest hole I had ever seen. He just disappeared. I took a half-dozen quick paddle-fu back sweeps to alter my point of impact to approximately ten feet off the left of Bruce's line, avoiding the heart of the hole. I was back-endered and flipped. I went into a tight tuck to protect myself, waiting to get oriented and to roll. The problem was that I never surfaced—that is, I was doing a mystery move upside down in my Dancer XT. After waiting approximately five seconds, I started to think about punching out; however, I never had a chance.

"Suddenly, I was being slammed from all sides by the most turbulent, powerful water that I had ever experienced. I was violently ripped, separated from my boat. I opened my eyes, expecting to see light of day—instead, I encountered nothing but silent, brown darkness. I think I had my paddle in my right hand though I'm not sure, but at that point, I just started dog-paddling. My eyes were darting around, searching for signs of light to orient myself. Nothing but brown darkness everywhere. I couldn't even see my hands. Only once, for a second or two, did I think I was going to die.

"After dog-paddling for what seemed an eternity (that actually in real time was probably no more than ten seconds), I thought, 'Maybe I'm paddling in the wrong direction, maybe I should dive for the bottom'—that is, if I knew where the bottom was. I didn't have any sensation that I was making progress. I felt suspended in time. Just then my head broke the surface, without warning. I went straight from darkness into the beautiful light. I don't remember my first breath. I don't remember gasping for air. What I remember was thinking, 'I've got to get out of this wave train; I've got to get to the shore.'

"As I paddled to the shore, I noticed that my life vest had been completely unzipped while I was submerged. The only thing that had kept it on was the waist ties at the bottom. Should I take time to rezipper the vest or just swim like hell to get off the river? I kept swimming and entered the tree line. Trees everywhere, with water flushing through, carrying me along. I was headed right for a small tree—a nice, clean tree trunk. At first my instinct told me to grab the tree, but then Nealy cartoons started flashing in my brain, pictures of kayakers eating tree trunks in flood-stage rivers, followed by the image of a kayaker pitoning on a tree with his feet. Resisting the strong urge to grab the tree, I brought my feet up to meet the tree trunk. With a hard push, I directed myself toward the right bank, out of harm's way. I managed to stand up in still water and climb up to the bank. I stood there, stunned, scanning my body to make sure I was all there, in one piece.

"I could see R. B. and Bruce Hayes working their way out of the water on river left. Then I heard moaning and turned to my left, behind me, to see Dave Jordan crawling out of the water, twenty yards upstream of me. Gasping for air, he asked if I was okay. Still bending over, he made the sign of the cross on his chest. We closed the distance between us and hugged each other, glad to be alive.

"Everyone was now accounted for except Leon. Where was Leon? Dave and I started bushwhacking downriver. We found Leon's yellow Dancer approximately one hundred yards downstream, wrapped end to end at the level of the cockpit, which was facing downstream. At first, we thought Leon was still in his boat. Realizing that wasn't the case, we continued searching for the missing boater. No success. We decided to walk out, back to the put-in, a mile or so upstream, hoping that Leon would turn up. On the way back, we spotted R. B.'s boat, floating in a thicket, upright and intact. We grabbed his blue Reflex and carried it out. When we arrived back at the put-in, no one was there. Hitching a ride with a bystander who happened to witness the river carnage, we proceeded downriver, this time along Highway 321, paralleling the Watauga. To our collective relief, Leon was with Bruce and R. B. He had stayed with his boat and was unable to break out of the wave train until he finally decided to swim for shore, abandoning his boat to the current and trees.

"Everything everyone said was entering my mind in a staccato fashion, piecemeal. Leon had dislocated his left shoulder; R. B. had hyperextended his legs. For the most part, there was quiet; few words were actually spoken, just a lot of long, somewhat empty stares. Everyone seemed to be off in his own little world, reflecting on his own unique experience.

"How could five experienced class IV-V boaters be so cavalier as to get on a flood-stage river that no one really knew, especially at that level, which probably was an all-time high, with only the one simple statement 'It will be a flush'? Speaking only for myself, in retrospect, I guess I had an attitude (though I never would have admitted it to myself or expressed it to others openly) that I couldn't be touched. I had a bomb-proof roll (onside and off), a solid combat hands roll, plenty of nasty hole experience with good escape techniques, and experience on both tight, technical and big, class IV-V water. I was competent. This near miss has definitely put things in proper perspective. No more brown-water runs on unfamiliar streams that can't be scouted. No more leaping without looking. I hope to be a much more cautious boater in the future.

"Epilogue: To date, July 7, 1989, three days after the event, four boats and two paddles have been recovered, three of the boats, including my own, having wrapped on trees."

It is sobering to think just how similar Fred's story is to many earlier accounts in this book, especially sobering to realize that what makes this one different, the only thing, really, is that everyone lives. Consider. On a flood-stage river, five boaters swim out of a horrible hole; four make it to shore near one another downstream. They split up to look for the fifth. He might be fine; he might be dead. Some might call discovering him, injured but safe, miraculous.

Some have also used that word to describe the save in the following account. Maybe even more than on the Watauga, luck played a role. But first aid skills on the part of the other boaters made the difference.

Lincoln Williams

In June 1990, four expert local paddlers were running a section of the Arkansas River in Colorado known as the Numbers. The run is fast and continuous and, at a gauge reading of 4.7 feet, solid class IV. All four paddlers put boating at the top of their life's priorities, paddling in excess of 150 days a year. They had just completed rapid number five and were within a quarter-mile of their take-out when an empty boat came past. Looking back upstream, they saw that the boater was on shore and okay. One of the boaters, Tom Karnuta, chief instructor of the Rocky Mountain Outdoor Center, continues the tale.

"The river at this point is very continuous, and as the four of us took off after the kayak, we knew we would be in for a long chase. As we chased the boat, we all noticed that a throw rope was attached behind the seat of the kayak. During the chase the knotted end of this rope came loose from the bag and seventy feet of rope was trailing in the river, still attached to the kayak. Several facts are important to note at this point:

1. The loose end of the rope had a large loop knot in it.
2. The bag end of the rope was still attached to the kayak.
3. All seventy feet of rope had paid loose from the bag.
4. All four of us were aware of the above situation.

"We chased the boat through very continuous class III+ water, with virtually no eddies for about half a mile. At this point, Greg and I were ahead of the boat and eddied out on river right. Looking upstream from this large eddy we could see Tim and Lincoln moving with the boat towards our location. At our position in the eddy the river constricts a bit, forming several large waves in the main current.

"Just above us the boat got away from Lincoln and moved out into those waves. Lincoln quickly made a move back towards the boat, which was in the center of the river, directly across from Greg and me in the eddy. At this point Greg and I were both in the process of peeling out of the eddy; Tim was slightly upstream. Lincoln, moving very quickly and precisely, was about to make contact with the bow of his boat on the loose kayak. As Lincoln positioned his bow against the loose kayak, the front of his boat, a fiberglass racing boat, passed under the rope from the throw bag.

"The rope was totally invisible to all of us at this time, with the knot of the rope lodged in a rock somewhere upstream very close to its maximum length. As Lincoln paddled into the unseen rope, it tangled around his paddle and his upper right arm. Lincoln gave a short yell as the rope quickly extended to its maximum length, pulling him and his boat underwater. It is important to visualize Lincoln's position at this time:

1. His body was completely submerged.
2. The rope was around his right biceps and the paddle shaft.
3. Lincoln was facing into the current, allowing his life jacket to remain in place.
4. He was positioned in the center of the river, directly in a large, violent wave.

"We took quick action to extend a throw rope across the river in an attempt to snag Lincoln. Unfortunately, our rope was not long enough. We had just finished running gates upstream and had only one rope, a fifty-foot kayak bag.

"Lincoln's wooden paddle, attached to his arm by the rope, was being violently snapped up and down with the pulsating wave. By some stroke of luck the paddle shaft broke in half, allowing Lincoln to slide free of the rope. We noticed his blue life jacket some fifteen yards downstream and quickly pursued it. (Approximate time lapse at this point was four to six minutes). As I approached, I thought it was only Lincoln's life jacket, but upon reaching it I found Lincoln still in the jacket, facedown, on his stomach, extremely cyanotic. I held Lincoln's head up out of the water in an attempt to reopen his airway and with great effort by Greg moved Lincoln through extremely continuous class III water towards shore.

"Tim and I immediately began CPR; Greg went to call the ambulance. It is important to remember that the water was cold. We kept Lincoln's body close to the water the entire time we administered CPR—approximately forty-five minutes—while waiting for the ambulance. Lincoln regained a weak pulse and started breathing on his own just as the EMTs arrived. Oxygen was immediately administered, and Lincoln was transported to Salida Hospital and then airlifted to Colorado Springs. There he made a complete recovery over the course of several weeks, and he's back on the water as I write."

Because of the danger that they will become caught, some boaters stuff throw bag loops completely inside the bag for security. Also, knotted loops on the free end of throw-bag ropes are sometimes removed by some boaters. This alteration makes the free end a bit harder to find but reduces the chance of an entanglement like Lincoln suffered.

Epilogue

This book makes for grim reading. We are reminded that potentially fatal accidents can happen unexpectedly to any of us. Careless boaters and careful paddlers may suffer the same fate. Despite heroic rescue efforts, some boaters die. Some live because they are lucky. Danger is are a part of whitewater. Let us all hope that, whatever our choices, we are blessed in our moment of greatest need with such remarkable luck and such competent friends.

Take from these accounts the lesson that no matter how skilled and careful you are, there is room to be yet more skilled and careful. No matter how much fun you are having, never forget that the forces you are dealing with are greater than you. Every moment on the river, when all is well, is precious.